THE LADY IN QUESTION

BY

CHARLES BUSCH

SAMUEL FRENCH, INC.
45 WEST 25TH STREET   NEW YORK 10010
7623 SUNSET BOULEVARD HOLLYWOOD 90046
LONDON   TORONTO

Copyright © 1989, 1990 by Charles Busch

ALL RIGHTS RESERVED

CAUTION: *Professionals and amateurs are hereby warned that THE LADY IN QUESTION is subject to a royalty. It is fully protected under the copyright laws of the United States of America, the British Commonwealth, including Canada, and all other countries of the Copyright Union. All rights, including professional, amateur, motion pictures, recitation, lecturing, public reading, radio broadcasting, television, and the rights of translation into foreign languages are strictly reserved. In its present form the play is dedicated to the reading public only.*

The amateur live stage performance rights to THE LADY IN QUESTION are controlled exclusively by Samuel French, Inc., and royalty arrangements and licenses must be secured well in advance of presentation. PLEASE NOTE that amateur royalty fees are set upon application in accordance with your producing circumstances. When applying for a royalty quotation and license please give us the number of performances intended, dates of production, your seating capacity and admission fee. Royalties are payable one week before the opening performance of the play to Samuel French, Inc., at 45 W. 25th Street, New York, NY 10010; or at 7623 Sunset Blvd., Hollywood, CA 90046, or to Samuel French (Canada), Ltd., 80 Richmond Street East, Toronto, Ontario, Canada M5C 1P1.

Royalty of the required amount must be paid whether the play is presented for charity or gain and whether or not admission is charged.

Stock royalty quoted on application to Samuel French, Inc.

For all other rights than those stipulated above, apply to George Lane, William Morris Agency, Inc., 1350 Avenue of the Americas,NYC 10019

Particular emphasis is laid on the question of amateur or professional readings, permission and terms for which must be secured in writing from Samuel French, Inc.

Copying from this book in whole or in part is strictly forbidden by law, and the right of performance is not transferable.

Whenever the play is produced the following notice must appear on all programs, printing and advertising for the play: "Produced by special arrangement with Samuel French, Inc."

Due authorship credit must be given on all programs, printing and advertising for the play.

ISBN 0 573 69166 5   Printed in U.S.A.

Dedication

This play is dedicated with gratitude and deep affection to the memory of Robert Vandergriff.

No one shall commit or authorize any act or omission by which the copyright of, or the right to copyright, this play may be impaired.

No one shall make any changes in this play for the purpose of production.

Publication of this play does not imply availability for performance. Both amateurs and professionals considering a production are *strongly* advised in their own interests to apply to Samuel French, Inc., for written permission before starting rehearsals, advertising, or booking a theatre.

No part of this book may be reproduced, stored in a retrieval system, or transmitted in any form, by any means, now known or yet to be invented, including mechanical, electronic, photocopying, recording, videotaping, or otherwise, without the prior written permission of the publisher.

IMPORTANT BILLING AND CREDIT REQUIREMENTS

All producers of THE LADY IN QUESTION *must* give credit to the Author of the Play in all programs distributed in connection with performances of the Play and in all instances in which the title of the Play appears for purposes of advertising, publicizing or otherwise exploiting the Play and/or a production. The name of the Author *must* also appear on a separate line, on which no other name appears, immediately following the title, and *must* appear in size of type not less than fifty percent the size of the title type. In addition, the following credit must be included in all programs:

"Originally produced by WPA Theatre, New York City, 1988 (Kyle Renick, Artistic Director)"

The Lady in Question was originally produced by the WPA Theatre, Kyle Renick, Artistic Director, and subsequently moved to the Orpheum Theatre under the auspices of Kyle Renick and Kenneth Elliott, under the direction of Kenneth Elliott, with set design by B.T. Whitehill, costume design by Robert Locke and Jennifer Arnold, wig design by Elizabeth Katherine Carr, and lighting design by Vivien Leone, and with the following cast, in the order of appearance:

Voice of the Announcer	James Cahill
Professor Mittelhoffer	Mark Hamilton
Heidi Mittelhoffer	Theresa Marlowe
Karel Freiser	Robert Carey
Professor Erik Maxwell	Arnie Kolodner
Hugo Hoffmann	Andy Halliday
Baron Wilhelm Von Elsner	Kenneth Elliott
Gertrude Garnet	Charles Busch
Kitty, The Countess of de Borgia	Julie Halston
Augusta Von Elsner	Meghan Robinson
Dr. Maximilian	Mark Hamilton
Lotte Von Elsner	Andy Halliday
Raina Aldric	Meghan Robinson

Logo Design ©1988 B. T. Whitehill

Cover Photo T.L. Boston

CHARACTERS

Voice of the Announcer
Professor Mittelhoffer
Heidi Mittelhoffer
Karel Freiser
Professor Erik Maxwell
Hugo Hoffmann
Baron Wilhelm Von Elsner
Gertrude Garnet
Kitty, the Countess de Borgia
Augusta Von Elsner
Dr. Maximilian
Lotte Von Elsner
Raina Aldric

SUGGESTED DOUBLING

In the original stage production, several of the roles were doubled which gave the actors in question wonderful opportunities to show their versatility. In the case of Meghan Robinson, who created the roles of Augusta and Raina Aldric, the doubling resulted in several very quick changes and provided her with a tour de force. I strongly recommend keeping these roles doubled:

Raina/Augusta
Hugo/Lotte
Professor Mittelhoffer/Dr. Maximilian

TIME: 1940

PLACE: The Bavarian Alps, outside the train station at Ludwigshafen, and the Schloss of the Baron Von Elsner.

AUTHOR'S NOTE

For the past few years, I've been in an incredibly fortunate position. I've had the opportunity to realize many of my more outrageous daydreams. In 1984, Ken Elliott and I started our company, Theatre-in-Limbo, since then as writer/performer I've been able to go back in time to swinging mod London, ancient Sodom, Malibu Beach circa 1952, and old Spain among others.

In the fall of 1988, we were asked to do a show for the WPA Theatre. I've always had a great fondness for Hollywood anti-Nazi war melodramas of the 1940's. I'm also a delirious fan of the late star, Norma Shearer. The result was *The Lady in Question*. So you see, I'm not lampooning these films such as *Escape* or *Above Suspicion* or *Notorious*, I'm saluting them. I'm celebrating a time in our country when issues weren't so muddy. There was an indisputable villain and it seemed as if indeed God was on our side.

Therefore, in performing this play, it is important not to "camp" it up and make the characters ridiculous. The style of the piece should be almost exactly the tone of those dark, grey suspense films — only slightly askew. Emotions run a bit too high, tough tootsies are a bit too hard-boiled. The audience must not for a moment lose the sense of urgency and pace that all traditional suspense plays should have.

I wrote the role of Gertrude Garnet to be played by myself in drag. I played it very realistically, or rather realistically in the grand manner of the star ladies of the past. I tried to create my own kind of star, but incorporated echoes of Bette Davis, Rosalind Russell, Barbara Stanwyck and of course Norma Shearer.

I see no reason why a woman couldn't play Gertrude Garnet most effectively. I honestly don't think there is a single joke that depends on gender role-reversal. The part of Lotte was also played by a fella, and he doubled as Hugo in the opening of the play. Andy Halliday played Lotte with great integrity and was hysterically funny because he was truly terrifying.

And that really is my point. If you play it right, this is one show where you can have your strudel and eat it too. You can keep the folks laughing and also make them hope you don't get shot in the keyster before the curtain falls.

PROLOGUE

A large four-paneled screen covers the width of the stage. It is a giant sized travel folder with the title "Tour Carefree Bavaria." The mood is dark, grey ominous. Lush movie SOUNDTRACK MUSIC is heard full of drama and triumph. The MUSIC quiets down to a feeling of suspense. A voice over of a sonorous, old time announcer is heard.

VOICE OVER. The year is 1940. Adolph Hitler's armies make his dream of European annexation a reality. Norway, the Netherlands, Belgium and France all fall before the monstrous power of the German fighting machine. Fear of fifth columnists makes idle chatter a thing of the past, as people across the continent live in terror.

(During the voice over, KAREL, a handsome, young Nazi stormtrooper goosesteps across the stage and exits.)

VOICE OVER. Nowhere is this more evident than in Hitler's own Bavaria. Free speech and free travel are but a distant memory, and those attempting to escape look with sad eyes to their local train terminal as a desperate symbol of hopes and dreams passing by.

(*The SOUNDS of a train pulling into the station are heard as the LIGHTS come up on Act I, Scene 1.*)

ACT I

Scene 1

The train station at Ludwigshafen. Afternoon. PROFESSOR MITTELHOFFER, a kindly, mildly eccentric old man awaits the train from Paris. With him is his daughter HEIDI. She is in her early twenties, very pretty, courageous and something of an emotional spitfire. Her fierce temper belies her fragile, Dresden doll appearance.

PROFESSOR. Heidi, I hope we have not missed his train. You should have woken me earlier from my snooze.

HEIDI. Papa, don't be silly. We're early. Professor Maxwell is arriving on the 11:58. And besides, you needed your rest. You've been slaving over your new translations for weeks.

PROFESSOR. "The Complete Letters of Thomas Jefferson." How Germany needs his wise words today.

HEIDI. How Germany needs her great men today. True greatness and not this (*With gutteral fierceness.*) revolting imitation of ...

PROFESSOR. Shhhh, Heidi! You must control your passionate nature. You inherited that from your mother, may she rest in peace.

HEIDI. Do you miss her terribly?

PROFESSOR. Very much so. (*HE sneezes.*)

HEIDI. Oh Papa, why are you not wearing your muffler? How many times have I told you?

PROFESSOR. I must have left it where I left my spectacles.

HEIDI. (*Takes his glasses out of her pocket.*) Here are your spectacles. I was wondering when you'd miss them.

PROFESSOR. My little mischief-maker.

HEIDI. What am I to do with you? Sometimes I feel like I am your wife. I like that feeling, Papa. I love you more than anything in the world. I'd kill for you.

PROFESSOR. That is not good, liebchen. A young girl must have her own life. I do not want you to develop an Elektra complex.

HEIDI. Papa, I promise you I won't.

(*KAREL, a handsome young stormtrooper, enters.*)

HEIDI. Look, Papa, there's Karel.

PROFESSOR. Heidi, don't ...

HEIDI. Hello, Karel!

KAREL. (*Comes over.*) Heidi, Professor Mittelhoffer, Heil Hitler.

PROFESSOR. Good morning, Karel.

KAREL. It is customary in the new order to reply "Heil Hitler."

PROFESSOR. You must forgive me, my lumbago.

HEIDI. (*Flirtatiously.*) Karel, it's been so long since we've ...

KAREL. (*Ignoring her.*) Professor, what brings you to the terminal so early?

PROFESSOR. I am meeting a colleague.

KAREL. A foreign colleague?

PROFESSOR. As a matter of fact, yes.

KAREL. From what country?

PROFESSOR. I am not aware of his citizenship.

KAREL. (*With mounting intensity.*) Why does he keep this a secret?

PROFESSOR. I imagine it is his choice.

KAREL. He has no choice. Why is he in Germany?

PROFESSOR. To gaze at our lovely alpine scenery?

KAREL. Do not treat me like a fool! I am no longer your pupil. No more can you make me sit in the corner with a dunce-cap. I would not want to report your activities to my superiors.

HEIDI. Karel, you must not speak to my father that way.

KAREL. Your father is a renowned intellectual, a loathsome species, and therefore under suspicion. It is my duty to leave nothing unnoticed.

HEIDI. (*Flirting.*) Then you've been shirking your duties.

KAREL. I have not.

HEIDI. You haven't noticed my pretty new frock.

KAREL. It is most becoming.

PROFESSOR. Excuse us. We must see if the train is late.

HEIDI. Oh, Papa, why don't you check?

PROFESSOR. Heidi, my ...

HEIDI. Go, go, go.

PROFESSOR. Heidi!

HEIDI. Go.

(*The PROFESSOR exits.*)

KAREL. Your father, he does not like me.

HEIDI. No one likes little boys with bad manners.

KAREL. I obey the code of the new order.

HEIDI. Karel, I've missed you.

KAREL. You can see me whenever you choose.

HEIDI. I miss the boy I once loved so dearly. I'm afraid he no longer exists.

KAREL. Heidi, don't.

HEIDI. I miss the boy I tutored every day. Your face was so cute when you'd strain for the simplest answers. For ten points: Name three tragedies by William Shakespeare.

KAREL. Shakespeare is dead. There is only Schiller and Goethe.

HEIDI. (*Grabs his head.*) Look at me! How do I crack open that big, good-looking, dumb head of yours? How do I let in some truth?

KAREL. (*Reciting.*) Adolf Hitler is our savior. The Third Reich will last a thousand years.

HEIDI. (*With wildly fierce emotion.*) Shut up and look at me! How do I make you feel, feel something! Anything! For chrissake, be a human being!

KAREL. (*Breaking into passion.*) I am a human being, Heidi, and I do love you, and I'm scared for you. Do not fall back with the malcontents. They will all perish. There is still a place for you in the Hitler Rhinemaiden brigade.

HEIDI. I wouldn't play canasta with those goose-stepping lezzies.

KAREL. (*Hardened.*) I see we are both not the young people we once were.

(*PROFESSOR MITTELHOFFER enters with PROFESSOR ERIK MAXWELL, a handsome American. HE carries a suitcase.*)

PROFESSOR. Heidi, our guest has arrived. We must go.

KAREL. Do not hurry, Professor. I should like to officially greet your esteemed colleague.

PROFESSOR. Professor Maxwell, this is my daughter, Heidi, and my former student, Karel Freiser.

ERIK. I'm flattered that I merit an official greeting. (*Puts down suitcase, Stage Left.*)

HEIDI. Your train was exactly on time.

ERIK. Yes, it arrived with frightening German efficiency.

KAREL. You will become accustomed to our well-organized society.

ERIK. It is a lovely country, the land of beer, Wagner and terror.

PROFESSOR. (*Nervously.*) He means terriers, schnauzers, dogs.

KAREL. My English is not fluent. Of course, English is a gutter language, ultimately to be extinguished.

ERIK. (*Matter of factly.*) While it's still spoken, up yours, asshole.

KAREL. I do not comprehend. Was heisst "asshole?"

ERIK. It means your Führer.

PROFESSOR. Take my word, Karel, in America, it is used most selectively. Come, you must be hungry.

KAREL. One moment. What is your business here in Germany?

ERIK. It is my business and none of yours, bub.

KAREL. Perhaps it should be the business of the prefect of police. Enjoy your visit, Professor, and let us hope it will be brief. Heil Hitler. (*HE looks at Heidi and exits.*)

ERIK. A graduate of Hitler's charm school.

HEIDI. It is foolish to bait him, Professor Maxwell.

ERIK. Forgive me. It was foolish, foolish and selfish. My big mouth will only reflect on you. I'm very sorry.

HEIDI. Your bitterness is understandable.

ERIK. I'm beside myself with worry. Since I received your letter, I haven't slept a wink. How is she? Have you spoken to her? Has there been any word?

PROFESSOR. Yes, there has been word. Can you take it?

ERIK. I can take it.

PROFESSOR. Your mother is to be executed on Friday.

(*ERIK starts to swoon, THEY catch him.*)

PROFESSOR. Buck up, my friend.

ERIK. (*With rapid-fire delivery.*) The monsters! I could kill every one of them with my bare hands. Why should they want her dead? She's an actress. She knows nothing about politics. Dead! That word has nothing to do with my mother. My mother is life, life itself! Why? Why?

PROFESSOR. I have known your mother a great many years. She is a brilliant actress, but "careful" is not a word in her vocabulary. She befriended a young, radical playwright, the hope of the German theatre. (*Embarrassed.*) It was rumored they became lovers.

ERIK. (*With a deadpan no-nonsense air.*) Professor, let me tell you right now, my parents divorced when I was little. My father was awarded custody and my mother returned to Europe where she has lived her own life. I do not judge her. Please go on with your story.

PROFESSOR. Using her legendary name, they mounted a production of the young man's most fiercely anti-Nazi play. On the opening night, the S.S. raided the theatre, killed the playwright and arrested your mother on the grounds of treason. She is in a prison a few miles away.

ERIK. This is a nightmare!

PROFESSOR. You will wake up, my friend, and soon. We have devised a plan of escape.

ERIK. Escape? Is it possible?

HEIDI. Yes, but exceedingly dangerous.

PROFESSOR. The plan involves the formidable figure of the Baron Von Elsner.

ERIK. Who is this man?

HEIDI. A decadent nobleman who has risen high in the Nazi regime. There are terrible tales of his numerous depravities.

ERIK. (*With genuine highminded interest.*) Spare me nothing.

PROFESSOR. Later, but for our plan to succeed, we need a confederate planted in the Baron's ancestral home. You can see it looming darkly in the mountains.

ERIK. What does the Baron's house have to do with my mother? None of this makes sense.

HEIDI. (*Urgently.*) You must do exactly as my father says.

ERIK. Of course, I trust you both completely. How do I find an ally in the Baron's home?

(*HUGO enters. HUGO is an intense highstrung fellow in his thirties. A touch of Peter Lorre.*)

PROFESSOR. That I do not know, but the escape must take place tomorrow night.

HEIDI. Papa, there is Hugo Hoffmann.

PROFESSOR. Hoffman is a noted painter. He has used his gift to forge letters of transit. If we are lucky enough to get your mother out of prison, we will need them to cross the border. He has made four of them. Be careful what you say. There are ears everywhere.

HUGO. Professor, how good to see you. (*Under his breath.*) I'm afraid the Baron Von Elsner may be on to my activities. (*Looking at Erik.*) Is this the one?

HEIDI. Yes, our friend has many contacts in the theatre and would like to see your sketches.

ERIK. Yes, I'm sure they will travel well in America.

HUGO. Compliment my tie. I will give it to you. Protest, then accept it. The letters of transit are inside the fabric.

ERIK. I do so admire your necktie.

HUGO. Then you must take it as a souvenir of our great country.

ERIK. You are far too generous.

HUGO. No, I insist. (*Takes off his tie and gives it to Erik.*)

HEIDI. The Baron.

(*BARON VON ELSNER enters. The BARON is a dignified, imposing man in his forties, a cold-blooded killer but with a silky charm.*)

BARON. Could that be the very talented Hugo Hoffmann?

HUGO. (*Terrified.*) Baron, this is an honor.

BARON. I must commend you on the restoration of my frescoes. Most skillful.

(*The rest of this scene is underscored by tense, suspenseful MUSIC.*)

HUGO. Thank you, Baron Von Elsner.

BARON. However, your latest creative endeavor disturbs me.

HUGO. The mural at City Hall? It is most reverential.

BARON. You are very clever. It took careful observation, but then I discovered it.

THE LADY IN QUESTION

HUGO. I don't know what you mean.

BARON. The magnificent detail surrounding the figure of the Führer is actually a code. A call to arms to your ridiculous resistance movement.

HUGO. That is not true. Perhaps someone has tampered with my painting.

BARON. That could be possible. Come with me to the prefect's office so we can clear up this misconception.

HUGO. By all means. Some traitor has defaced my work. Herr Baron, if I could stop and use the facilities, I'd be most grateful.

BARON. Of course, Hugo, of course.

(HUGO starts to make a run for it. KAREL enters to block his way. HUGO turns to the Professor.)

HUGO. Help me, help me, please.
PROFESSOR. What can I do?

(HUGO jumps off the front of the stage and makes a run for it.)

BARON. Halt! Halt in the name of the Führer!

(BARON shoots Hugo in the back. HUGO falls down, dead beyond the view of the audience. HEIDI screams. The BARON and KAREL

exit. ERIK, the PROFESSOR and HEIDI are horror-struck and hurry away. ERIK leaves his suitcase Stage Left. The LIGHTS dim.)

VOICE-OVER. Yes, human life is cheap in the fatherland. The time has come for all men to come to the aid of humanity, to cast off self interest and band together. But, as always, there are SOME PEOPLE who ignore the cataclysm around the. SOME PEOPLE who live only for their hedonistic pleasure. SOME PEOPLE WHO DON'T GIVE A GOOD GODDAM FOR ANYONE BUT THEIR OWN STINKIN' SELVES!

(The glamorous, internationally acclaimed American concert pianist, GERTRUDE GARNET* enters, having just arrived on the Paris train. SHE's elegantly dressed in a traveling suit and furs. SHE speaks in a grand, very affected manner that disguises her honky tonk background. At this moment, SHE's in a terrible snit.)

GERTRUDE. Where is she? Where is my maid? Suzette! Suzette! If that dreadful girl thinks she can leave me high and dry without my cosmetic bag, she's got another thing coming.

---

* Pronounced GAR-NAY.

(*Looks around.*) Conductor! Conductor! Where is everyone? Kitty! Kitty!

(*KITTY, THE COUNTESS DE BORGIA, enters. KITTY is Gertrude's long-time buddy from her vaudeville days. Kitty is an attractive blonde, wisecracking, tough as nails but with a heart of gold. Now married to a nobleman, Kitty, too, can affect a high tone when it's required.*)

KITTY. Hold your horses, Gertie. These gams are still moving on Palm Beach time.

GERTRUDE. This is absolutely appalling. How could Suzette do this to me? Quitting without even giving notice.

KITTY. You shouldn't have slapped her across the face with that paillard of veal.

GERTRUDE. I was making a point.

KITTY. You sure made it. The dame jumped off a moving train.

GERTRUDE. I never dreamed she'd be so vindictive. Fleeing with my cosmetic bag. The lashes alone are worth over a thousand dollars. Why are there so many soldiers about with their great scowling faces?

KITTY. Honey, I say we get back on that train and skip this part of the tour.

GERTRUDE. (*Aghast.*) Skip this part of the tour? Kitty my recitals in Munich, Frankfurt, and Ludwigshafen were scheduled four years ago and are completely sold out.

KITTY. Give 'em back their money and let's beat it. This whole country gives me the creeps.

GERTRUDE. Kitty, I am an artist, the leading concert pianist on the international stage and when Gertrude Garnet says she'll appear, she appears, hands oiled and ready. Where is the car from the hotel?

KITTY. (*Laughs.*) You know, Gertie, this reminds me of our old vaudeville days when we were left stranded in Altoona.

GERTRUDE. Kitty, this is hardly the time.

KITTY. We were booked on the same bill as that slimy escape artist.

GERTRUDE. He was a mentalist. Is that the car?

KITTY. Whatever, he escaped with the cashbox.

GERTRUDE. (*Becomes her tough former self.*) And because you gave him the romantic fisheye, the manager thought we was in cahoots.

KITTY. I never gave him the fisheye.

GERTRUDE. Ah, you were dropping them eyelids like they were a fire-curtain. And that stingy manager, he was as tight as Kelsey's nuts. (*Regains her soignee tone.*) Kitty, I am not in the mood for strolling down memory lane.

KITTY. Well, you should. You've become just too hoity-toity since you took up that egghead music.

GERTRUDE. That egghead music has paid off in spades.

KITTY. I still say you were a lot happier when we were in vaudeville and I played fiddle to your honky-tonk piana.

GERTRUDE. Now you're a wealthy countess. I hardly see you renewing your union cards.

KITTY. Sister, after having the Count de Borgia rubbing his old sausage on me, gimme a split week in Pittsburgh.

GERTRUDE. Stop that. We've risen to the top of high society and do you know how we made it?

KITTY. Behind a lot of wives' backs.

GERTRUDE. No, because it was our destiny. I've been seeing the most marvelous mystic, so wise, and terribly profound.

KITTY. Not another one. That last holy man gave me one helluva goose.

GERTRUDE. Not the swami. He's laid out for me the entire blueprint of life. He calls it his New World Philosophy. Every thing that happens to us happens because we make it happen. There was no luck involved in my career. (*With a rather frightening hard edge.*) I made my luck.

KITTY. So you mean somehow we wanted to be stranded in this train station?

GERTRUDE. Indeed. Perhaps instinctively we know that some great adventure lies in store for us. You see, darling, the rhythms and patterns of millions of years of civilization have brought you and me to this very moment. Now it remains for us to choose how we're going to handle this occasion. We *can* change the pattern.

KITTY. (*Not impressed.*) Change the tune, girl, the record's got a scratch on it.

GERTRUDE. Stop that, Kitty, this is important.

KITTY. I just have trouble believing that if our train had crashed, it would have been because I chose it.

(*ERIK enters and as he passes the ladies on his way to get his suitcase, HE can't help hearing what they are saying.*)

GERTRUDE. Entirely possible. Sometimes I think all these people who say they're being persecuted, perhaps they chose it too. Unconsciously, of course. It does make it rather hard to sympathize, though, doesn't it?

ERIK. That is the stupidest hog wash I've ever heard.

GERTRUDE. (*Haughtily.*) I beg your pardon!!??

ERIK. That half-baked philosophy is extremely dangerous.

GERTRUDE. (*Aside to Kitty.*) Kitty, he's a nut, move over. (*Pulls Kitty over a bit Stage Right.*)

ERIK. Open your eyes, lady. Innocent people are disappearing around you. The Nazis are planning to tattoo people to separate them from the rest of us. There are stories of hideous camps built to isolate those out of political favor.

GERTRUDE. *(Blithely.)* Such an alarmist. Besides, we all have many reincarnations. This one may be dreary, chances are the next one will be all champagne and caviar.

ERIK. One day, you're going to be shaken out of this foolishness and I'll feel very sorry for you.

GERTRUDE. Sing no sad songs for me, darling. Come, Kitty.

ERIK. You're famous, aren't you?

GERTRUDE. Extremely famous and extremely bored.

ERIK. You're Gertrude Garnet, the pianist. *(Pronounces her name like the birth stone.)*

GERTRUDE. Gertrude Garnet. *(Garnay.)*

KITTY. You're an American. Are you here for work or amusement?

GERTRUDE. Kitty.

ERIK. I have important work in Germany.

KITTY. I hope it won't take up all of your time.

GERTRUDE. *(To herself.)* I can't believe I'm waiting out here without a car.

ERIK. Where are you staying?

GERTRUDE	KITTY.	ERIK.
We're staying with friends.	The Hotel ...	I don't mean to pry.
Kitty, don't ...	The Hotel Mitzi.	I thought perhaps we...

ERIK. The Hotel Mitzi. I read about that in the newspaper. Yes, it was confiscated last week. When the concierge protested, he and this entire staff were executed.

KITTY. How dreadful.

GERTRUDE. Dreadful indeed. It's Octoberfest and we'll never find another reservation.

(*The BARON enters.*)

KITTY. What are we going to do?

(*GERTRUDE approaches the Baron and asks him, in German, where she can find a hotel.*)

GERTRUDE. *Mein Herr, mein Herr, entshuldigen Sie bitte, mein Herr. Meine Freudin und ich suchen Unterkunft.*

BARON. I speak English, Madame Garnet.

GERTRUDE. (*Pleased.*) Oh.

BARON. I would recognize you anywhere. I am the Baron Von Elsner. (*Attempts to take her hand, SHE withdraws it.*)

GERTRUDE. (*Laughing.*) I'm afraid I never let anyone touch my hands. They're insured by Lloyds of London.

BARON. (*With great charm.*) I can well understand. I have many of your recordings in my home. Your boxed set of Schubert is a particular favorite.

GERTRUDE. The German composers are so good for the fingers. Have you heard my Beethoven "Appassionata?"

BARON. It haunts me. I'm particularly fond of your Schumann "Fantasy Stucke,"

GERTRUDE. Oh, and this is my traveling companion, the Countess de Borgia.

BARON. (*Takes her hand.*) And are your hands insured?

KAREL. (*Coldly.*) Just personal liability.

BARON. (*With veiled irony. To Gertrude.*) Your friend is very amusing. (*To Kitty.*) You must visit our local circus. Unfortunately, our leading clown was mauled to death by an angry lion. I have not been introduced to your other friend.

GERTRUDE. We just met him.

ERIK. Professor Erik Maxwell.

BARON. And your field of expertise?

ERIK. Nutrition. I'm making a study of German dietary habits.

BARON. Yes?

ERIK. I believe there is a connection between the heartiness of German beer and bread and your legendary ambition.

BARON. We do eat well, but you must not forget, we are the master race. Now, my dear Madame Garnet, you were asking me something.

GERTRUDE. The Countess and I are in terrible straits. We had reservations at the Hotel Mitzi, and now I heard it's closed. Could you recommend some first-class hostelry?

BARON. The Mitzi was a dreadful place. May I offer you the use of my Schloss?

KITTY. Come again.

GERTRUDE. His Schloss, dear, his villa. We couldn't possibly accept.

BARON. It is quite lovely, right on the lake at Shauffehausen.

KITTY. I've never been inside a real German slush.

GERTRUDE. Schloss, dear. Perhaps we could spend the night, until we find further accommodations.

BARON. Delighted. Professor Maxwell, you must join us for dinner. I find your theories most intriguing.

ERIK. I will be there. Goodbye, ladies.

KITTY. Then we'll see you later at the Baron's schnapps.

GERTRUDE. Schloss, dear.

KITTY. Right.

ERIK. Till then. (*He exits.*)

BARON. Shall we go? I'll have my manservant collect your luggage.

GERTRUDE. Just those thirty-seven pieces. This is such a lovely surprise. Baron, I simply can't wait to see your magnificent shlong. I mean, schloss! (*Mortified by her blunder.*)

(*THEY all exit.*)

(*BLACKOUT.*)

(*Wagner's "Liebestod" is heard in Liszt's piano transcription. As the action moves into the next scene that evening, the MUSIC becomes Gertrude's playing in the adjoining salon.*)

ACT I

Scene 1

The Schloss of the Baron Von Elsner. That evening. The ski lodge has been the Von Elsner's vacation home for generations and reflects their malevolence in its cold, grey austerity. A grotesque boar's head is their notion of whimsical decor. There is a front door USC and a fireplace DSL. Above the fireplace is a portrait of Hitler. A large sofa Center Stage is the only furniture. A staircase starts USR and goes to a landing above the front door. There are two doors on this landing. Downstairs SR there are two doors. One to the kitchen (large swinging door) and DS of that door is the door to the concert room. On SL above the fireplace an archway leads to the library. We hear Gertrude playing the PIANO in the concert salon. KAREL enters the front door with the very elegant BARONESS AUGUSTA VON ELSNER. White haired and magnificent, she is the Baron's mother. Her aristocratic charm masks an evil, cold spirit.

AUGUSTA. Ah, how grand to be home. Thank you, Karel, for escorting me from the train.

KAREL. It is my honor, Baroness.

AUGUSTA. (*With grandeur.*) This solid entry bids me welcome and gives me strength. Indeed, no one would dare invade my portal. My, what lovely playing. Is that a new recording?

KAREL. The Baron is giving a party and the American pianist, Gertrude Garnet, is the guest of honor.

AUGUSTA. (*Somewhat disturbed.*) An American? How very interesting.

BARON. (*Enters from the salon.*) Mother, you've arrived, looking splendid. We've missed you. (*Removes her cape.*)

AUGUSTA. I arrived home a day early and a grand soirée is in progress.

BARON. (*Gives cape to Karel.*) An intimate supper party, nothing more. Karel, you may go.

KAREL. Yes, your excellency. (*Hangs cape in closet next to front door and exits.*)

BARON. Now, Mother, tell me of your visit to Heidelberg.

AUGUSTA. Who is this American piano player?

BARON. Gertrude Garnet is a world famous artist. She is to perform at the Festspielhaus next Tuesday. Madame Garnet and her friend, the Countess de Borgia, will be staying with us.

AUGUSTA. The Countess, an Italian?

BARON. No, she too is an American.

AUGUSTA. (*Thinking it over.*) Two Americans under our roof?

BARON. Yes, and they are charming ladies. Come, Mother, you must hear Madame Garnet play.

AUGUSTA. Two Americans under our roof? Willy, is this prudent?

BARON. I see no reason why it should not be.

AUGUSTA. My dear son, we shall be at war with their country at any moment. What could you be thinking of? I am astonished. The Führer will not find this to his liking.

BARON. (*Exploding.*) Mother, I will not be bullied by you or the Führer, do you hear me? (*Stamps his foot.*)

AUGUSTA. Wilhelm!!! Don't you dare raise your voice to me, not in my house!

BARON. (*Meekly.*) Forgive me, Mother.

AUGUSTA. After you have finished entertaining these creatures, you will find them accomodations in the village for the night.

BARON. (*Quietly.*) Mother, that I cannot do.

AUGUSTA. Willy, is there something you're not telling me? What is it? You and I have no secrets. We are partners, soldiers in arms.

BARON. Madame Garnet ... I am in love with her.

AUGUSTA. Willy.

BARON. I have met her but this morning and I am passionately in love.

AUGUSTA. You cut a ludicrous figure. You are not a school boy with an idiotic infatuation. You are a commanding officer, serving the greatest leader in the history of the world. Now straighten your back and remember your duties. I shall telephone the Inn and find these women lodging.

(*SHE picks up the telephone on the mantle. The BARON stops her.*)

BARON. You don't seem to understand, Mother. I plan to marry her. She shall be the next Baroness Von Elsner.

AUGUSTA. (*Puts down the phone receiver. With great intensity.*) Wilhelm, if you persist in this foolishness, before all the servants ...

BARON. I do not wish to argue. Have you never fallen in love at first sight? Of course you have, my darling, beautiful Maman. Surely with Father.

AUGUSTA. Indeed not. The marriage was contracted at birth. You should know. For centuries the Von Elsners have married their first cousins.

(*The MUSIC ends, we hear APPLAUSE.*)

BARON. Please, Mother, do not be rude to her.
AUGUSTA. I am never rude.

(*GERTRUDE enters in a magnificent evening gown. She is followed by KITTY, ERIK and DR. MAXIMILIAN. The Doktor is an elegant Nazi aristocrat in his forties. HE, KITTY and ERIK carry drinks.*)

DOKTOR. Brilliant, simply brilliant, so passionate and yet so effortless.

GERTRUDE. This is, of course, the secret to playing Wagner. One must and I say, one must, read his score as one would read Shakespeare. The notes themselves always dictate the emotion. (*To Augusta.*) Dear, I left my drink on the piano.

(*To the Doktor.*) When I first approach any score, I look ...

BARON. Madame Garnet, this is my mother, the Baroness Von Elsner.

DOKTOR. Augusta, we did not expect you until tomorrow.

AUGUSTA. Evidently, Doktor Maximilian. I see you have taken time off from your medical experiments.

DOKTOR. It has been well worth it. I only wish you had arrived earlier to partake of Madame Garnet's genius.

AUGUSTA. I am sure we will hear more from Fraülein Garnet before her visit is over.

BARON. (*With a note of warning.*) *Mutter, Du hast versprochen, Dich gut zu benehmen.* (Mother, you promised you would behave.)

AUGUSTA. (*Disgusted.*) *Was siehst Du in Ihr? Sie ist so vulgaer and buergerlich.* (What do you see in her? She is so vulgar and common.)

BARON. *Mutter, beleidige Sie nicht. Ich warne Dich.* (Mother, do not embarrass her. I'm warning you.)

AUGUSTA. *Drohe Deiner Mutter nicht.* (Do not threaten me.)

GERTRUDE. (*Oblivious.*) Love your hair. What would you call that color?

KITTY. Battleship grey.

BARON. Mother, the Countess de Borgia and Professor Maxwell.

ERIK. A pleasure.

AUGUSTA. Another American. *Ach du lieber.* Has our country been invaded in my absence?

BARON. Mother is quite comical. You know the German sense of humor.

(*GERTRUDE laughs gaily then abruptly stops when SHE realizes there was nothing funny.*)

AUGUSTA. Madame Garnet, forgive my ignorance of your remarkable career. As chairwoman of the Reich Committee for the Preservation of the Teutonic Arts, I have devoted myself to the work of exclusively German artists. Do you include any Strauss in your repertoire?

GERTRUDE. (*With charm.*) Indeed. His "Bein Schlafengehen" is a concert staple of mine.

AUGUSTA. (*Appalled.*) An American playing "Bein Schlafengehen." No doubt you also perform his "Burlesque in D."

GERTRUDE. (*Understands the bitchiness behind the remark.*) I sure do. I'm also quite adept with Liszt, particularly his "Weiner, Klager, Sorgan, Zagen."

AUGUSTA. (*Topping her in bitchiness.*) Really, of course, a true test would be Schumann's "Warter, Warter, Wilder, Schiffsmann."

GERTRUDE. (*The war escalates.*) I play it with my eyes closed. Honey, get me in the right mood, and I'll hit you with my "Faschingsschwank aus Wein!"

AUGUSTA. I am sure you do quite a raucous "Freulings Fahrt!!"
GERTRUDE. (*Mad.*) Oh, yeah!

(*LOTTE, the Baron's teenage niece, appears at the top of the stairs. With blonde braids, elaborate traditional German costume, she is a twelve-year-old demon.*)

LOTTE. (*Scampering down the stairs.*) Uncle, uncle, why did the pretty music stop?
BARON. Lotte, what are you doing up so late?
LOTTE. Uncle Willy, I heard the music. It was ever so lovely.
BARON. Madame Garnet, my niece Lotte.
GERTRUDE. Perfectly charming.
AUGUSTA. Madame Garnet and her friends are from America.
LOTTE. America. That dreadful place, so dirty, so crowded. All the races mixed up. (*To Kitty.*) You have such a funny face. Doesn't she have a funny face? You must be a combination of a million races.
KITTY. I sure am, honey, but you're pure bitch.
GERTRUDE. Kitty, that's a terrible thing to say.
KITTY. It must be this German firewater. I apologize, dear.
AUGUSTA. You will find Lotte quite precocious. She has a great interest in history.

DOKTOR. She knows far more than I do.

LOTTE. (*With perverse enthusiasm.*) Oh yes, I practically live at the prison museum. Do you know they have a complete fourteenth century dungeon. They have a rare torture device whereupon four prongs are attached to the prisoner's face and then stretched in four different directions.

KITTY. A totalitarian face lift.

BARON. Shall we have coffee in the library? Cook brews an excellent cafe Viennese, and we will have some chocolates.

LOTTE. May I come, Uncle? I love sweets.

BARON. May she, Mother?

AUGUSTA. All right, but do not overindulge. Chocolate gives you acne.

(*SHE exits, MAXIMILIAN follows.*)

KITTY. (*To Lotte.*) Oh, don't worry, honey, tomorrow we'll find you a nice medieval pimple popper.

(*SHE exits, followed by LOTTE, then ERIK. The BARON stops Gertrude.*)

BARON. Gertrude, this has been such a delightful surprise, meeting you.

GERTRUDE. And you were a godsend. I really don't know what we would have done.

BARON. I only wish I could spend more time with you. I have so many meetings and military obligations. I hope you won't find our little village too tiresome.

GERTRUDE. Oh no, I adore *quiet* places.

BARON. Away from the glamor of Manhattan?

GERTRUDE. Rather.

BARON. Away from the many stage door Johnnies. Isn't that what you call them?

GERTRUDE. (*Amused.*) Yes, that's what we call them.

BARON. I imagine a woman of your fame and beauty has many, how do I say, flirtations?

GERTRUDE. Fewer than you may think. I'm completely devoted to two figures, the bass and treble clefs. (*Sits on sofa.*)

BARON. Is there no place in your life for love? (*Sits beside her.*)

GERTRUDE. I'm not too keen on love, never having known it. Besides, my spiritual advisor, the swami, has made me realize that I can't love others until I love myself first. I must be number one. And I can only make others happy after I have made myself completely happy, first and foremost. It may take years.

BARON. You're very mysterious, Gertrude. As mysterious as a prelude by Debussy.

GERTRUDE. Am I? (*SHE plays piano scales on her arm of the sofa.*)

THE LADY IN QUESTION 43

BARON. Such beautiful hands. Let me see them. Ah, lovely. So delicate. (*SHE displays her hands in a picturesque manner.*)

GERTRUDE. Yes. Every finger is double-jointed and X-rays have revealed large airpockets in the bone marrow.

BARON. So sensitive and yet so practical. Rather like myself. I feel as if we were two melodies that fit together in perfect counterpoint.

GERTRUDE. I'm flattered, your excellency.

BARON. Your excellency? Why so formal? You Americans are so famous for your nicknames. What shall you call me?

GERTRUDE. (*Flirtatiously.*) Well, for Wilhelm, I could call you "Bill." And, of course, you are a bit older than I, I could call you "Popsie."

BARON. No, I don't care for that. What about "darling?"

GERTRUDE. Don't you think that's a bit too intimate?

BARON. (*Rises. Intimately.*) No, I don't. And to demonstrate our intimacy, I shall let you in on a little secret. I'm going to show you something of mine I don't let everyone see.

GERTRUDE. (*Dubious.*) Oh, yeah?

BARON. You see that portrait of the Führer?

GERTRUDE. An excellent likeness.

BARON. (*Pulls it away, revealing a safe.*) It conceals a safe. Most clever. Everything of importance is locked in that safe. Let me see if I can remember the combination. Now, close your eyes.

(*SHE does. HE murmurs the combinations, SHE mouths it to remember.*)

BARON. Turn right three times to zero, left all the way round to six, right back to twelve. Open sesame. Voila!
GERTRUDE. (*Stands and crosses to Baron.*) Whatcha got in there, Billy boy?
BARON. All sorts of goodies. This ring once belonged to the Grandduchess Mathilde.
GERTRUDE. Ooh, daddy, emeralds.
BARON. (*Gives her ring.*) It looks lovely with your hair. Try it on.

(*SHE puts on the ring.*)

BARON. Most attractive. It's yours.
GERTRUDE. I couldn't possibly ...
BARON. Please, it gives me pleasure, but for now, when you see Mother, turn the ring around.
GERTRUDE. By all means.
BARON. (*Silly.*) And there's more where that comes from, baby. But only for the girl that I marry.
GERTRUDE. Mmmm, you're tempting me. And all in that safe?
BARON. No, no, no, no. They are in a special vault. The most precious object in this safe is this

set of keys. The keys to every room in the house and for the rooms off the catacomb.

GERTRUDE. The catacomb?

BARON. The house was built in the fifteenth century. My warrior ancestors built a mile-long network of tunnels leading away from the house as an escape route.

GERTRUDE. And where does it end?

BARON. A nasty place. Let's not speak of it, particularly when these keys lead to such nice places, such as the vault where we keep the family jewels. (*Returns the keys and locks the safe.*) Now, my darling, does that illustrate our intimacy and my trust?

(*ERIK enters.*)

GERTRUDE. I promise I won't betray it.

BARON. Ah, Professor Maxwell, do come in.

ERIK. I don't wish to intrude.

BARON. You did, but you are forgiven. Gertrude, I must check on Mother. She was away for the weekend and I haven't even asked about her trip. She can be a real Tartar when she feels ignored. Will you miss me?

GERTRUDE. Unendurably.

BARON. My darling. (*Exits.*)

ERIK. You two get along very well.

GERTRUDE. He's sweet.

ERIK. Like a tarantula.

GERTRUDE. (*Warning.*) He is our host.

ERIK. I must apologize for my rudeness this morning. I was a busybody and deserved the treatment I got.

GERTRUDE. I, too, was at fault. But with my maid running off and the loss of our hotel reservation, I really was at sixes and sevens.

ERIK. Then friends?

GERTRUDE. Friends.

ERIK. It sure is good hearing an American voice. I like talking to you, even beefing with you.

GERTRUDE. A good fight does wonders for the circulation.

ERIK. Then I must be in excellent health. I'm afraid I'm not adjusting very well to the German way.

GERTRUDE. Really, I wonder why. It couldn't be more lovely. And the people are so warm, so friendly, so, how do they say it, "gemutlich."

ERIK. Haven't you noticed the fear in everyone's eyes?

GERTRUDE. Fear? What are they afraid of?

ERIK. Miss Garnet, surely you read the newspapers. Germany is in the grip of an evil dictator. The whole country's gone mad. Such arrogance. I tell you, I've had it up to here. (*HE raises his arm in a "Heil Hitler" salute.*)

GERTRUDE. I never, never discuss politics. I am an artist, the world is my stage. Now what else can I do for you?

ERIK. I can't help feeling we've met before.

GERTRUDE. When you're a great celebrity, you find this happens quite often.

ERIK. It was on the stage, but not in a concert hall. Where could it have been? My God, it was in a beer hall ...

GERTRUDE. (*With forced gaiety.*) A beer hall?

ERIK. ... a beer hall in ... Sandusky, Ohio ...

GERTRUDE. I hardly think ...

ERIK. ... Nearly fifteen years ago. You weren't wearing much either ...

GERTRUDE. (*Indignant.*) Now really ...

ERIK. Now I remember, didn't you used to be Barrelhouse Gertie, the Kissing Kitten on the Keys?

GERTRUDE. (*With vulgar roughness.*) Oh, shut up.

ERIK. Then I am correct?

GERTRUDE. (*Tough and common.*) So what of it? I never said I was an overnight success. Okay, Charlie Chan, what's your angle?

ERIK. I'm hoping to find underneath your glamorous facade, the real woman.

GERTRUDE. What for?

ERIK. Because I must ask her a deep favor.

GERTRUDE. (*Irritated.*) Now it comes. How much do you want?

ERIK. I don't ask this favor for myself, but for someone I love very much; my mother. It's dangerous for me to speak to you here.

GERTRUDE. Spill it now.

ERIK. My mother, my mother is also a great artist, an actress, her name is Raina Aldric.

GERTRUDE. (*Impressed.*) Raina Aldric is your mother? I saw her on the stage when I was very young, a great actress. How can I be of any help to her?

ERIK. (*Bitterly.*) As we speak, she lies dying in a Nazi prison only a mile away.

GERTRUDE. A prison so near by.

ERIK. A prison for political prisoners. My mother was arrested for appearing in a play that dared speak against the new order. For this hideous crime, she is sentenced to death.

GERTRUDE. That poor woman.

ERIK. But in a mad world, sometimes one can succeed with a mad act.

GERTRUDE. (*Nervously.*) What are you saying?

ERIK. I have friends here, brave wonderful people who have planned her escape tomorrow. I can't tell you the details now, but there is one fatally missing link. We need an ally here in the Baron's home.

GERTRUDE. (*Breaking away from him.*) You mustn't ask me this.

ERIK. I beg you, please help me.

GERTRUDE. I dare not.

ERIK. Please. Please.

GERTRUDE. (*Frightened.*) I'm a simple, ordinary woman, extraordinarily talented, perhaps, but in every other way, ordinary. I am not capable of such heroism.

ERIK. Then you're a coward, a selfish, egocentric, opportunistic, vulgar, manipulating cunt!

GERTRUDE. Vulgar! Now that did it. Look here, you. I don't owe you or your old lady anything. I pay my own freight, never asking for a handout. Now, you must excuse me. I must join my host, the Sacher torte is said to be divine.

ERIK. Yes, gobble down their Nazi food, guzzle their Nazi wine, and try to sleep tonight.

GERTRUDE. You go too far.

ERIK. (*Grabs her.*) Please help me, I don't even know what I'm saying anymore. I'm desperate. You are our only hope. If you don't help us, Raina Aldric will die on Friday. Please, please help me! (*SHE breaks away from his grasp.*)

BARON. (*Enters.*) I seem to be interrupting a passionate scene.

ERIK. I was demonstrating a new method to save someone from choking.

BARON. She will have no need of that. I hope you have enjoyed yourself, Professor Maxwell. I have done my best to be hospitable. Food and intelligent conversation, my favorite pastimes.

ERIK. And at times, equally hard to swallow.

BARON. Not in my house. We all tend to think the right ideas.

ERIK. Or rather, forced to think the right ideas.

GERTRUDE. (*Alarmed.*) Erik!

BARON. (*Intrigued.*) Erik? You have become quite intimate.

(*A STRAUSS WALTZ is heard in the salon.*)

BARON. Professor, I don't think I like you. I shall remember this evening. (*To Gertrude.*) My darling, they are playing a Strauss waltz. Will you indulge me in a spin, if my impudent friend will permit?

(*Terribly torn, GERTRUDE looks first at Erik, then at the Baron. THEY form a triangle. SHE makes her choice and crosses vivaciously to the Baron.*)

GERTRUDE. But, of course. A waltz can be marvelously diverting.

(*The MUSIC swells, the BARON leads Gertrude in a waltz. HE moves her in a circle but as SHE spins around to face the audience, the look on her face is one of agonized guilt.*)

(*LIGHTS fade to black.*)

ACT I

Scene 3

The MUSIC fades out. LIGHTS UP and we are in the catacomb below the Schloss. It is morning. A backdrop is in that shows the catacomb in it's creepy, black, dank state. HEIDI is garbed as a prison guard. With her in a wheelchair is the legendary RAINA ALDRIC. Raina is a beautiful woman in her fifties, fragile but still dramatically vibrant. SHE lives on drama and speaks in the manner of a wildly flamboyant stage actress.

HEIDI. That was close. I was sure the guard saw through my disguise. You may rest now, Madame Aldric. For the moment, you are safe.

RAINA. Safe. The most beautiful word in any language. But where am I? What time of day is it? I'm so bewildered.

HEIDI. You poor darling. It's early morning. A short while ago, I moved you out of the prison infirmary, took you through the secret door and we came down that very long tunnel. We are now in a room off that tunnel and directly underneath the home of the Baron Von Elsner.

RAINA. A baronial home. I do not understand.

HEIDI. The Baron's ancestors built two fortresses, one they lived in and the other was a prison. They linked them together with a long series of catacombs in case of enemy attack. That door leads to the interior of the Baron's home and to freedom.

RAINA. Why are we waiting? We should go through it now.

HEIDI. The door is locked from the outside. We must wait till my father or Erik opens it and escorts us through the house late tonight.

RAINA. (*With great theatricality.*) Freedom! I shall never be free. I have seen too much and I shall never be free of the memories. They have destroyed me. I no longer even have the will to walk.

HEIDI. You are a great actress. You have so much more to give.

RAINA. I was once was a great actress. "The shining beacon of the European stage" was what Brecht once called me. "Aldric's Hilde Wangel sang with a poetry Ibsen could only hint at," *Munich Bugle,* September 9. 1934. "Raina Aldric's Ranyefskaya ranks with the Cathedral of Chartres as one of the world's great artistic treasures," *Lisbon Daily News,* May 12, 1937. But now I'm old, weak, my legs are worn-out pipe cleaners. You should have let them execute me. My soul died the night they shot my lover, Gebhardt. "Don't shoot him, don't, don't shoot!" Bang, bang, bang. "Then kill me too, kill me!"

(*HEIDI bursts into tears.*)

RAINA. (*Concerned.*) Forgive me, I didn't mean to upset you.
HEIDI. No, it's just that I, too, was once in love.
RAINA. Is he dead?
HEIDI. He might as well be. His name was Karel, the most wonderful boy in the world. It seems a century ago that we lay in the weinerwald and he taught me the names of all the birds and flowers that gathered about us.
RAINA. What happened?
HEIDI. He came under the influence of the Baron Von Elsner. They have turned his brains to sauerkraut. When I look into his beautiful eyes, I only see swastikas. (*Weeping vulnerably.*) Madame Aldric, tell me, help me understand why he has turned against me. (*With fierce, hardened vengeance.*) Oh God, how I hate them. They've made this whole goddam world LOUSY! Well, something has changed in Heidi Mittelhoffer and I'm gonna make those bastards pay for what they've done. They've butchered my dreams!!!

(*KITTY and GERTRUDE, laughing, are heard Offstage, unlocking the door.*)

GERTRUDE. (*Offstage.*) Kitty, this has got to be the right key.

KITTY. (*Offstage.*) Gertie, give it a break.

GERTRUDE. (*Offstage.*) I wanna see those family jewels if it's the last thing I do. I didn't open that damn safe for nix. (*Opening the door.*)

HEIDI. Someone's coming.

KITTY. I gotta sit down. This tunnel is as long as Gary Cooper's ...

(*THEY see Raina and Heidi.*)

KITTY. Oh, I'm so sorry.

GERTRUDE. We're guests of the Baron. We were having a marvelous time exploring his lovely home.

KITTY. We didn't mean to intrude.

GERTRUDE. (*To Heidi.*) You were at the train yesterday, weren't you?

HEIDI. Yes, I was meeting my father.

KITTY. Your friend looks ill.

HEIDI. No, she's quite all right.

KITTY. She's pale as a ghost and trembling. She should see a doctor.

RAINA. Thank you for your concern. I'm recovering from an illness.

KITTY. Your voice is so familiar. Are you an actress?

RAINA. Oh no, never.

KITTY. Of course you are. Why, you're Raina Aldric.

GERTRUDE. (*Shocked.*) Raina Aldric. But I thought you were ...

HEIDI. Please, please, you must pretend you've never seen us.

KITTY. What do you mean?

GERTRUDE. Kitty, we should leave this place and do as she says.

KITTY. Are you a guest of the Baron's? But why are you in this drafty, cold room? Come, we'll take you upstairs where it's warm.

HEIDI. No, you mustn't.

RAINA. Please, I am quite all right. (*SHE has a sudden attack of pain in her heart.*) A toothache.

KITTY. This is silly, you must come with us.

GERTRUDE. Kitty, Madame Aldric is a prisoner of the Nazis. I believe this young woman has engineered her escape.

KITTY. This is utterly mad. How do you know of this?

GERTRUDE. Eric Maxwell told me and he ... he is her son.

RAINA. Erik, you know my Erik?

GERTRUDE. Yes, I do.

RAINA. You must be the one. The ruby red hair. A gift from heaven.

GERTRUDE. It's actually a gift of henna.

RAINA. You are the one in my dream. I have a recurring dream that my Erik is walking through the snow with a beautiful young woman with long red hair. I know in my heart, she is the woman he shall marry.

GERTRUDE. I hardly know him.

RAINA. I feel it in my heart. (*SHE has another heart attack.*)

GERTRUDE. He's really quite a guy. Come, Kitty, we should return before our absence draws attention.

KITTY. Was Erik enlisting your help? He was, wasn't he?

GERTRUDE. Yes, he was.

KITTY. (*Very gung ho.*) Why didn't you tell me? What do we do? How do we proceed?

HEIDI. You must forgive me. I didn't know you had agreed to help.

RAINA. You are both most gracious.

KITTY. Forget that. Just fill me in.

HEIDI. This morning, disguised as a guard, I moved Madam Aldric out of the prison, through the tunnel and into this room under the Baron's Schloss.

GERTRUDE. (*It all dawns on her.*) Yes, of course.

HEIDI. We are to remain here for eighteen hours, at which time, one of you will unlock this room and usher us through the house.

KITTY. Yes, and then?

HEIDI. At precisely midnight, a car will be waiting at the servants' entrance to drive us to the airfield and a plane which will fly us to Switzerland.

KITTY. Well, count me in.

GERTRUDE. Kitty, we must talk. You will excuse us.

KITTY. Let's run upstairs, and rustle up some blankets, hot coffee and crullers. Then we can ...

GERTRUDE. Kitty, stop it.

KITTY. Gertie, what's wrong?

GERTRUDE. Nothing.

KITTY. (*The light beginning to dawn on her.*) Gertie, I don't know, but I'm beginning to believe you refused Erik. You refused to help his mother. Tell me I'm wrong.

GERTRUDE. (*To Raina.*) We'll get you some crullers ...

KITTY. You did refuse him, didn't you?

GERTRUDE. Please, Kitty, let's go upstairs.

KITTY. No, answer me. I want the truth.

GERTRUDE. Yes, I refused him. I'd botch it up. I'd be a hindrance.

KITTY. (*Quietly.*) That's not the reason, and you know it. (*Painfully.*) You're selfish, Gertie. All your life you've thought of no one but yourself.

GERTRUDE. This is hardly the time for a character analysis. (*Turns away from Kitty, her face obscured.*)

KITTY. I'm seeing you as if for the very first time. Oh, Gertie, your face has a terrible look to it.

(*GERTRUDE turns around, her face looks like a grotesque version of Ma Barker. SHE realizes this and tries to restrain it.*)

KITTY. Go ahead. I'm going to stay.

GERTRUDE. Kitty, you fool, this is serious business. This isn't a madcap caper with your Palm Beach eccentrics. If the Nazis catch you aiding the escape of a prisoner, you'd be lucky merely to be shot.

KITTY. We just won't fail. Besides, I'm not a citizen of Germany.

GERTRUDE. No, but all your finances are tied up in Italy. I've read enough to know that Germany and Italy are allies. You could lose your entire fortune.

KITTY. Sister, with this face, I'll never starve. Now, are you going to help?

GERTRUDE. No, I can't. Nothing personal, Madame Aldric, but I'm scared. Scared to death. I'm not courageous. I like a warm, comfortable bed, a fur coat, dinner and dancing at the Stork Club. I'm not cut out for self-sacrifice. I'm leaving. I must put in my three hour's daily practice, I have a concert at the Festspeilhaus on Tuesday. I shall pretend I never opened this door. Kitty, will you join me? Kitty?

(*KITTY leaves Gertrude and goes over to Raina and Heidi.*)

GERTRUDE. Very well. But please, do be careful. (*SHE exits and we hear a door close.*)

KITTY. Madame Aldric, do not fear, we shall bring you to safe harbor.

(MUSIC comes in, tender and somewhat sad. It slowly builds as we watch the three women in tableau. The LIGHTS FADE TO BLACK.)

ACT I

Scene 4

The Schloss. An hour later. KITTY enters, looks around furtively, and goes to the telephone. SHE takes a cigarette from a box on the mantle and lights it with a lighter.

KITTY. *(To the operator.) Hallo, Telephonistin, sprechen Sie Englisch? Koennten Sie mich bitte mit jemandem verbinder, der die Sprache spricht?* (Hello, operator, do you speak English? Could you connect me with someone who does?) Thank you. Operator, please connect me to Felsenkirk. The number is Bitburg eight, four thousand. Thank you. Hello, is this the Professor? This is the Countess de Borgia.

(From her room at the top of the stairs, LOTTE comes out and quietly watches.)

KITTY. (*Unaware of Lotte.*) I'm calling the the Schloss of the Baron Von Elsner. I have seen Raina Aldric, and Heidi has told me all. I am willing to do anything I can to help ... Yes ... yes ... But of course ... Yes, I can do that. Goodbye. (*SHE hangs up, thinks for a moment, she picks up the phone again.*) Operator, the overseas connection ... Hello I would like to place a transatlantic trunk call to the United States ... Yes, thank you.

(*Very softly we start hearing SCARY MUSIC. LOTTE now starts down the stairs very quietly and slowly to hear better. SHE gets all the way to the bottom of the stairs before KITTY senses her.*)

KITTY. Hello, New York, please. The number is Trafalgar six, five one hundred ... Walter Winchell, please. The Countess de Borgia, and make it snappy ... Walter, darling, it's Kitty. I'm calling from Germany and, darling, the Deutschland is as dreary as a rotten bratwurst. I've got a scoop for you, but you've got to promise to keep it under your hat for a few days. Remember the German actress, Raina Aldric, well, I've just ... (*For the first time, KITTY feels Lotte's presence. Into phone.*) I've just ... I've just remembered that I left the number in my room. I'll ... I'll call you later. (*Puts out her cigarette.*)

THE LADY IN QUESTION 61

(KITTY hangs up the phone as LOTTE comes into the room. Slowly KITTY turns and sees Lotte. BOTH smile at each other..)

KITTY. Hello, Lotte.
LOTTE. I like your scarf. It's so pretty.

(SCARY MUSIC builds. LOTTE starts moving toward Kitty slowly as the LIGHTS FADE TO BLACK.)

ACT I

Scene 5

The SCHLOSS, an hour later. LOTTE is onstage holding Kitty's scarf from the last scene. SHE hears someone KNOCKING and hides it in the cushions of the sofa. KAREL enters, looking for someone.

KAREL. Good afternoon, Fraülein Von Elsner. (*Turns to leave.*)
LOTTE. Who were you looking for?
KAREL. The Countess. I am to drive her to the beautician in the village. (*Looks at slip of paper.*) Fritzi's Chalet of Beauty.

LOTTE. Well she changed her mind. She won't be needing the services of a beautician.

KAREL. Thank you, Fraülein, for the information. (*Turns to leave.*)

LOTTE. (*Blocks him.*) Don't go, Karel. I want to talk to you.

KAREL. Yes, Fraülein.

LOTTE. Why don't you call me Lotte? I've asked ya a dozen times.

KAREL. It would not be fitting. I am a soldier under your uncle's command.

LOTTE. Screw him. I want you to be my best friend.

KAREL. (*Nervously.*) I am your friend ... uh ... Lotte.

LOTTE. (*Caressing his chest.*) You know, you're not that much older than me, Karel.

KAREL. You're growing up very fast.

LOTTE. (*With dead seriousness.*) Very fast. I'm bleeding regularly.

KAREL. (*Trying to be encouraging.*) Congratulations.

LOTTE. (*Perversely flirtatious.*) I have a confession. I've never seen a man's weiner. Take it out, I want to see it.

KAREL. (*Appalled.*) No, Lotte.

LOTTE. Then give me a kiss.

(*SHE kisses him, HE wipes it off unconsciously.*)

LOTTE. Why did you do that for?

KAREL. What?

LOTTE. You wiped off my kiss.

KAREL. I didn't.

LOTTE. (*Moving into hysteria.*) You did. It's as if I repulsed you. You hate me, don't you?

KAREL. I don't.

LOTTE. You hate and despise me. Well, you'll be very sorry you wiped off my kiss. (*Viciously.*) Very sorry indeed!

(*The BARON and the DOKTOR enter.*)

BARON. Karel, are you waiting for me, what can I do for you?

KAREL. (*Panicked.*) I was to drive the Countess to the village, but I hear she has changed her mind. If there is nothing else, may I go?

BARON. But of course. Heil Hitler.

KAREL. Heil Hitler. (*Exits.*)

BARON. (*Furious.*) Those blundering idiots! How could a sick, old woman be allowed to escape?

DOKTOR. That sick old woman has strong allies. Do not worry, Raina Aldric's friends shall be rounded up and executed.

LOTTE. Uncle, I have already done ...

BARON. Death will be too mild. First, in the name of science, they will all be volunteered as subjects for your most extreme medical experiments.

DOKTOR. Science must be served.

LOTTE. Uncle ...

DOKTOR. Herr Baron, why is this case of such importance to you?

BARON. To the liberals, Raina Aldric is a great symbol of artistic conscience. That symbol must be crushed. Art must serve the nation.

DOKTOR. But, Herr Baron, who is to judge what is good or bad art?

BARON. (*Intrigued.*) Such questions, Herr Doktor. You are beginning to sound like a liberal.

DOKTOR. (*Alarmed.*) No, Baron, call me anything but not a liberal.

BARON. Decent people can judge what is obscene. All of the arts are mired in decadence. And the theatre is the worse. I am sick of effeminate neurotics parading their warped fantasies across our stages.

LOTTE. Uncle, listen to me. I have taken care of the little matter you spoke of. One of Raina Aldric's cohorts has indeed been disposed of.

BARON. (*Pleased.*) Lotte, my little bulldog. You have done well.

(*He roughhouses with her. SHE barks like a dog.*)

BARON. Bite the Doktor, bite the Doktor. Sic him, Lotte. Sic him.

(*SHE attacks the Doktor like a pit bull.*)

THE LADY IN QUESTION

DOKTOR. Lotte, stop!!! Please stop!!!

(GERTRUDE enters from the front door in riding clothes, brandishing a riding crop.)

GERTRUDE. *(Amused by the spectacle.)* Oh dear, I knew I should have packed a muzzle.

BARON. Liebchen, have you had a brisk canter?

GERTRUDE. *(Full of vigor.)* Bracing, invigorating. Have you seen Kitty? We're having our hair done together in the village.

BARON. I have not seen her.

LOTTE. I saw her this morning. She did not seem quite herself.

GERTRUDE. *(Placing her knee on the back of the sofa jauntily.)* Really, in what way?

LOTTE. She mentioned something about an albatross around her neck, choking her. What could she have meant?

DOKTOR. A most stimulating young woman.

BARON. We are going to the beer garden in the village. Care to join us?

GERTRUDE. No, thank you, I think I'll wait for Kitty.

BARON. You should not be alone. But, I imagine loneliness is a cloak worn by all artists.

GERTRUDE. It would take a special man to strip it off me.

BARON. (*Tantalized.*) Most provocative, Gertrude. Before long I shall find the key to your mysterious nature.

GERTRUDE. (*Suspicious of his intentions.*) The key?

(*THEY stare at each other for a beat.*)

BARON. Yes, the key. Till later. Auf wiedersehen, my sweet.

(*BARON, DOKTOR, and LOTTE exit into library.*)

GERTRUDE. Auf wiedersehen. (*SHE nervously takes the keys from her pocket, checks kitchen door, and tiptoes over to the safe. SHE swings the portrait open and attempts to open the safe.*) Turn three times to zero. Then the opposite way round to twelve and then back to six. (*It doesn't open.*) Oh, boy. It must have been left. Round to twelve ... no, it was six ...

AUGUSTA. (*Offstage from kitchen.*) No, Elsa I said "sauerbraten for six", not at six.

(*GERTRUDE quickly closes the portrait and puts keys back in her pocket and looks up at portrait as AUGUSTA enters, carrying a large book. SHE is surprised to see Gertrude.*)

AUGUSTA. Gertrude?

THE LADY IN QUESTION

GERTRUDE. I can gaze at this portrait for hours. Those eyes, so sensitive and yet so virile.

AUGUSTA. (*In rapture.*) What an honor to serve such a man. My only regret is that I am too old to bear him children.

GERTRUDE. There are other forms of volunteer work. Please, don't let me disturb whatever it was you were doing.

AUGUSTA. I was consulting my astrological charts. I find astrology a cruelly neglected science. What is your birthday, Gertrude?

GERTRUDE. August twenty-third. The cusp of Leo and Virgo.

AUGUSTA. A most revealing horoscope. (*Pronounced whore-scope.*)

GERTRUDE. (*Laughs.*) That's horoscope, Baroness.

AUGUSTA. (*Laughs.*) My English. Do forgive.

GERTRUDE. Of course.

AUGUSTA. I would imagine you are far closer to the lion than the virgin.

GERTRUDE. (*Catching her drift.*) No, I think I'm right in the middle.

AUGUSTA. A combination is rather interesting. One could be a ferocious prude or a methodical *tramp*.

GERTRUDE. (*Hardboiled to the core.*) Enough with the digs. You don't like me, do you? Why? (*SHE crosses to Augusta confrontationally.*)

AUGUSTA. (*Calmly.*) Because you are from a hateful, enemy nation. You are cheap and common, are using my son and embody everything I loathe in the human race.

GERTRUDE. (*Beat.*) Gimme another reason.

AUGUSTA. Fraülein Garnet, you are a guest of my son. I am doing my best to be gracious to you and your friend. By the way, where is the Countess?

GERTRUDE. (*Concerned.*) I don't know but I should like to find her.

AUGUSTA. (*Going upstairs.*) Do not worry. I am sure you will find her shortly, my dear. I suppose she could be almost anywhere. Good day. (*Exits - Lotte's room.*)

(*Feeling great anxiety, GERTRUDE sits on the sofa. SHE stretches her arms out and flings them down wide on the sofa. Accidentally, she touches Kitty's scarf tucked behind a pillow. Tense, suspenseful MUSIC underscores the rest of the action. Confused, GERTRUDE picks up the scarf. Determined to get to the bottom of Kitty's disappearance, she puts down the scarf and crosses to the Stage Left arch. SHE calls out "Kitty!" When there's no response, SHE crosses Center Stage and looks up to the landing and calls out "Kitty! " Still no response. Resigned, she slowly crosses to the Down Stage Right door, lost in her thoughts. SHE opens the door and to her*) *horror, KITTY swings out, hanging from a noose, her face hideously contorted. GERTRUDE screams. "What have those fiends done to you!" As Kitty continues to swing back and forth, GERTRUDE runs to the mantle to steady herself. In hysteria, SHE crosses back to Kitty and then collapses to the floor in a faint as the MUSIC builds to a climax and the LIGHTS fade quickly to black.)*

END OF ACT I

ACT II

Scene 1

The Schloss, several hours later. ERIK is comforting Gertrude. SHE suffers beautifully in a luxurious full length velvet dressing gown.

GERTRUDE. It was horrible. Her lovely face, so twisted, her eyes bulging.
ERIK. Here, take my handkerchief. Where is she now?

(HE gives her his handkerchief, SHE uses it and returns it to him.)

GERTRUDE. I must have fainted. When I came to, her body was gone. Thank you for rushing over so quickly. You must think me totally mad.
ERIK. I believe every word you've said.
GERTRUDE. How could they do this? She, who was so kind, so gentle.
ERIK. They'll stop at nothing until the whole world is filled with their evil.
GERTRUDE. (*Rises from the sofa.*) I must see the swami. He'll make sense of this. He says

everything happens because we choose it. I must take comfort in that.

ERIK. (*Challenging her.*) Then Kitty somehow wanted to die?

GERTRUDE. (*Cries out in confusion.*) I don't know! She couldn't. No one loved life more than Kitty. Erik, I'm so confused. It's as if the ribbon that's kept my world together has untied. You see, Kitty and I fought. She said I was selfish, that I think only of myself ... and Erik, she was so right. I've lived a terrible life and now, now I'm so ashamed.

ERIK. I'm sure she would have forgiven you.

GERTRUDE. That I shall never know.

ERIK. I imagine you'll be on the next plane.

GERTRUDE. No, I'm staying on.

ERIK. What do you mean?

GERTRUDE. I must avenge Kitty's death. She was my friend. I must finish the work she died for, saving your mother. The Baron and his henchmen knew of Kitty's pledge to aid your mother. That's why they killed her. Raina Aldric must leave Germany alive.

ERIK. Then you're with us?

GERTRUDE. If you'll have me. I'll cancel my concert at the Festspeilhaus. I'll whip up some excuse, but first I must see the Baron. I'll have it out with him. Force him to admit they murdered Kitty.

ERIK. No, you must pretend you never found Kitty.

GERTRUDE. (*Aghast.*) But Erik ...

ERIK. (*Forcefully.*) Listen to what I say. You can do us more good if the Baron continues to trust you.

GERTRUDE. You're asking me to pretend I'm in love with him. Aren't you?

ERIK. Yes, I am. It will act as a smokescreen to mask our true plans. Will you do this? Can you do this?

GERTRUDE. (*Revolted but game.*) Yes. You can depend on me. I shall carry out this deception to its very end. Can you ever forgive me for my foolishness? (*Tender, romantic MUSIC underscores the scene.*)

ERIK. Of course. You're so unbelievably beautiful at this moment. The way the sunset catches your face and hair.

GERTRUDE. Oh, you mean like this? (*Composing her face into an unforgettable image.*)

ERIK. (*With deadpan thoughtfulness.*) No, like this (*Adjusting the position of her head.*) I know it's madness to feel this way after so short a time and with so much at stake, but I love you, Gertie.

GERTRUDE. Please, don't say it.

ERIK. I love you. From the first moment I met you.

GERTRUDE. (*Tenderly.*) I believe you, and the strange thing is, I feel the same. For the first time, something has burst inside me and I feel what the poets call love. But do I trust it?

ERIK. You must and you will.

GERTRUDE. (*Tremulously.*) Erik, hold my hands.

ERIK. Really? I know how you feel about your hands.

GERTRUDE. It doesn't seem to matter anymore. Today, we all need as much tenderness as we can find. (*SHE takes his hands.*) Hold my hands like any American boy would do with his girl. They won't win, will they, darling, the Nazis?

ERIK. (*With inspiring fervor.*) We won't let 'em. God is on our side. Yeah, he's a regular Joe who won't let the bad guys get away with just a kick in the pants. You'll see, this time the krauts will be smashed to smithereens forever.

GERTRUDE. And will we be fighting alone?

ERIK. No, ma'am. All of Europe will join together. Uncle Sam'll come in swinging, and Russia too. Sure, the Nazis fooled 'em for awhile, but they've wised up. I met Joe Stalin once, at a seminar in Moscow. He wasn't so bad. Believe me, kiddo, he won't let old Schickelgruber into his backyard.

GERTRUDE. I love hearing you talk this way.

ERIK. I love holding you this way. (*HE gently kisses her.*)

GERTRUDE. Darling, we have so little time. Do you see that portrait? Behind it lies a safe. This morning, Kit ... Kitty and I opened it and found the keys to all the rooms in the house.

ERIK. Good going.

GERTRUDE. Unfortunately, when I tried to return them, I forgot the combination. I'm terrified the Baron will notice the keys are missing ...

ERIK. We can only hope he doesn't go near the safe for (*Looks at his watch.*) the next six hours. Let's fetch Mother from the catacombs.

GERTRUDE. I've seen to that already. I've hidden your mother and Heidi in the butler's pantry.

ERIK. You're a genius.

GERTRUDE. (*Radiantly.*) Go to her, darling.

ERIK. Mother on the other side of that door. It's been so many years since I've seen her. I've got the willies.

(*HEIDI wheels RAINA in from the kitchen.*)

RAINA. Erik?

ERIK. Mother?

RAINA. My darling. (*THEY embrace.*) I thought I'd never see you again. Look at you, so big, so handsome. You were a little boy when last I saw you.

ERIK. From now on, you'll never be alone.

THE LADY IN QUESTION 75

RAINA. My heart can't take such happiness. My dear, too many years have been wasted. Perhaps it was wrong of me to pursue the career I did, traveling around the world.

ERIK. You're a great artist.

RAINA. Yes, but I had a child. You must believe me, I wanted to take you with me, but your father, the son of a bitch, he thought it best that you grow up in a more normal, stable household. You don't hate me?

ERIK. Hate you? I worship you.

HEIDI. Come, we best hurry.

RAINA. Where do we go now?

GERTRUDE. Erik, you and Heidi leave. I'll take care of your mother for the few hours until the car arrives at midnight.

HEIDI. But I couldn't possibly leave her.

RAINA. Heidi, darling, you must do what Madame Garnet says. She knows best.

HEIDI. (*Near hysterics.*) But what if she has another attack, or starts to shake, or falls into a coma, or what if she ...

RAINA. Heidi —

HEIDI. Yes, ma'am.

GERTRUDE. I'll bring Madame Aldric upstairs to the attic. There is to be a supper party tonight and that should divert attention.

ERIK. It's like you're a different woman.

GERTRUDE. I am a different woman. (*With a swift gesture, she lifts Erik's coat and hat off the back of the sofa.*) Come, hurry.

ERIK. Mother, this shall be our last goodbye for a long time.
RAINA. God bless you.

(*THEY kiss.*)

HEIDI. Goodbye, Madame Aldric.
GERTRUDE. Godspeed.

(*SHE gives coat and hat to Erik. HE kisses her on the cheek. HE and HEIDI exit.*)

RAINA. He loves you, Madame Garnet.
GERTRUDE. (*Embarrassed.*) Oh.
RAINA. And you love him.
GERTRUDE. Oh.
RAINA. You're blushing.

(*GERTRUDE, blushing, makes a raspberry sound and puts her face against the wall.*)

RAINA. I'm a worldly woman. I know a great deal about love, particularly how to squander it.
GERTRUDE. We hardly know each other. What we may say now, in a moment of ...
RAINA. It can happen in an instant. Two people meet and their past and future are one. Don't end up like me, old, sick, alone. Look at this face, look at it. There's a lot of mileage on this puss. Every role I played, every dirty dressing

room, every mile I traveled is etched on this map. Look at it, my girl, this could be you.
GERTRUDE. (*Horrified.*) No! No!

(*THEY hear LOTTE BARKING from salon.*)

GERTRUDE. Oh my God, someone's coming. Hide behind the sofa.
RAINA. But I can't.
GERTRUDE. Get down. (*SHE pushes her out of the wheelchair and behind the sofa. The Downstage Right door to the salon opens, obscuring Gertrude as she pushes the wheelchair out the swinging kitchen door.*)
LOTTE. (*As SHE enters from the salon followed by the BARON.*) I hate her. I hate her.
BARON. (*Follows Lotte.*) But, Lotte, you will learn to love Madame — (*Turns as GERTRUDE shuts salon door.*) ... Ah, Gertrude! Are you alone in here? I thought I heard voices.
LOTTE. There were two female voices, Uncle.
GERTRUDE. I suppose I'll have to confess. I've been involved in a top secret project.
BARON. Indeed?
GERTRUDE. (*Madly improvising.*) I'm composing an opera. I was acting out all the roles. It's a very contemporary opera.
LOTTE. She's lying. Don't believe her.
BARON. Lotte, that was ill-mannered. Apologize to Madame Garnet.

LOTTE. (*Crosses to her.*) I love stories. Tell us the story of your opera.

GERTRUDE. Never you mind. It's very sophisticated, and I wouldn't want your hormones to go haywire. You're liable to wake up in the morning, full breasted and with a moustache. No, I'm dreadfully tired. I think I'll lie down here for awhile.

BARON. Wouldn't you be more comfortable in your own room?

LOTTE. (*Very bitchy.*) Uncle, I think Madame Garnet would like to be alone in this room. It's so dusty! That new servant girl is so incompetent. Let me do a quick cleanup of the *entire* room.

GERTRUDE. (*Rushing to Lotte.*) No! It was rude of me not telling you the story of my opera. Let's see. I'll act out the whole thing for you. Lotte, you sit over here. (*SHE pushes Lotte down on the sofa with such force that Lotte's skirt flies up reducing Lotte to a flurry of pink petticoats. To Baron.*) And you, darling, you sit over here. Nice and comfy. (*SHE gently seats him also on the sofa.*) This shall be the stage. (*SHE indicates the Downstage area.*)

(*SHE moves down near fireplace as RAINA's head pops up behind sofa.*)

GERTRUDE. It all takes place in Greenwich Village. That's part of New York. Downtown.

(*SHE sees Raina.*) No, what am I saying? I've changed it. It takes place in Harlem. That's uptown. Up, up, uptown.

(*SHE points for Raina to go upstairs.*)

GERTRUDE. It's the upper corner of Manhattan Island. The upper right corner.

(*RAINA drags herself up the stairs.*)

GERTRUDE. That's right, folks, Harlem. The home of Jelly-roll Morton, The Cotton Club, Satchmo.

(*SHE sits on arm of sofa next to the Baron, as RAINA starts up to the first landing.*)

GERTRUDE. It's about the wild, bohemian set. Grasping at everything life has to offer, one step at a time. This woman, Annabella, is a painter. A painter of large murals and loose morals. Isn't that funny? Sometimes I just come up with these little ... (*No one is laughing.*) She falls in love with a nobleman, kind of like you.
BARON. Like me?
GERTRUDE. Oh yes, handsome, debonair.
BARON. This nobleman; he makes her happy?
GERTRUDE. (*Near hysteria.*) Oh honey, she's downright slaphappy!

BARON. (*Amused.*) Then it must be, what you call, escapist entertainment.
GERTRUDE. You might say.
LOTTE. (*Standing up.*) I'm bored.

(*RAINA hides around corner of first landing, as GERTRUDE stands up and runs to Lotte holding an imaginary knife.*)

GERTRUDE. (*Screams.*) A crazy lady runs out of a building holding a knife. She sings "I can't, I can't. I can't go on much longer like this."

(*During this SHE has "stabbed" Lotte back down on the sofa again. RAINA falls from her hiding place onto the newel post of the second landing.*)

GERTRUDE. The music gets faster and faster. It speeds up, accelerato!

(*RAINA falls onto second landing stairs.*)

GERTRUDE. It slows down.

(*RAINA drags herself up to second landing.*)

BARON. (*Starting to get up.*) It's chilly in here . Let me close the window.
GERTRUDE. (*Pushing the Baron back onto the sofa.*) I didn't tell you, Annabella also works

as a part-time chiropractor. She met the Baron while cracking his neck.

(SHE sits between the Baron and Lotte and with one arm grabs the Baron around the neck to keep him from seeing Raina.)

BARON. Ow!
LOTTE. It *is* cold in here. I'll close the ...
GERTRUDE. *(With her other arm, grabs Lotte around the neck.)* She's also a part-time lesbian.
BARON. This sounds like decadent art.
GERTRUDE. Oh, it's madly decadent. Annabella seduces the Baron and his niece. She takes them to her artist's garret and forces them both to strip naked.

(Behind them on the top landing, RAINA realizes she simply can't walk another foot to get to the door. SHE does a full somersault that gets her to the exit.)

GERTRUDE. Slowly she caresses their nude bodies and ...

(GERTRUDE looks up and RAINA gives her the okay sign, and exits.)

GERTRUDE. And that's all I'm going to tell you. I'm fairly tingling with inspiration. I must go to my room and compose. (*SHE runs up the stairs at a clip.*)

BARON. But, Gertrude, what happens next?

GERTRUDE. I'm concentrating, darling. (*SHE sings strange atonal phrases as SHE ascends the stairs and exits.*)

LOTTE. The whole thing was a lie.

BARON. Lotte, you must not be so suspicious. Come, Lotte, let us go to the freezers and choose the best steaks and sausages for tonight's supper. (*THEY cross to the mantle. The BARON moves Hitler's portrait revealing the safe.*)

LOTTE. Oh, Uncle, this is an honor. You've never let me see the freezers before.

BARON. I keep my special keys in the safe behind this portrait. (*Does the combination.*) Now that you are a young woman, I shall trust you with these keys. (*Opens the safe, sees keys are missing.*) That's strange. The keys are missing.

LOTTE. (*Gasps.*) She took them! She took them! I thought I saw her sneaking around here this morning.

BARON. Who, Lotte?

LOTTE. The piano player, Miss Gertrude Garnet!

BARON. But why should she do this? She is in love with me. True, her friend was a conspirator, but not Gertrude, I don't believe it.

LOTTE. Uncle, only an hour ago I heard her arrange to meet the other American, Erik

Maxwell. Are you aware that Erik Maxwell is none other than the son of Raina Aldric?

BARON. (*Screams and starts to strangle Lotte.*) This is not true!!! (*Controls himself.*) Is true. What a great fool I am. What have I done?

AUGUSTA. (*Enters with basket of apples.*) Good afternoon, my liebchen. Why so glum? It is a gorgeous day.

BARON. Mutter, I have done a terrible thing. We must talk.

AUGUSTA. (*Fearing the worst.*) What have you done, Willy?

BARON. It is hard for me to say.

AUGUSTA. First, bring me a cigar. Then you will sit here and tell me what you have done. (*SHE sits on sofa, basket of apples to floor.*)

BARON. Mutter, I have fallen in love. (*Lights cigar.*) I have fallen in love with an American agent.

AUGUSTA. Is she with a big agency like William Morris?

BARON. You don't understand. She is a spy. Gertrude Garnet has helped Raina Aldric to escape.

AUGUSTA. (*Fiercely.*) Swine!!! (*Slaps him.*) Dumpfkopf!! Why do you not listen to me?

BARON. Mother, please.

AUGUSTA. You are weak, Wilhelm, weak. This is the eternal curse of the Von Elsners.

BARON. Please, Mother, not in front of Lotte.

AUGUSTA. No, she must stay. She is more of a man than you. Let her know of her heritage and the cross she must bear. All of the men in your ancient line have been weak, infantile. It is the women who have led the family to greatness.

BARON. That is not true. My father died a hero in battle.

AUGUSTA. Your father died in a madhouse. I should know. I placed him there. They all go the same way. First they display childlike stupidity, then impotence, and then madness.

BARON. (*Spooked.*) I am still not mad. I will show you, Mother. I will show you I am not weak. Fraülein Garnet!!!

AUGUSTA. Don't! I gather she does not know you know that she knows that we know.

BARON. Uh uh.

AUGUSTA. Then let us wait a bit longer.

LOTTE. And then I will strangle her myself.

AUGUSTA. No, Lotte, that would not look good. Such an important personage must not be found murdered. It must appear far more natural. I shall take care of the lady in question.

(*BARON cries, head in hands.*)

AUGUSTA. Do not worry, my little Wilhelm, Mother will take care of everything.

(*Bright Viennese waltz MUSIC comes in as the LIGHTS blackout and continues into the next scene.*)

BLACKOUT

ACT II

Scene 2

The Schloss, that evening. GERTRUDE, DOKTOR, BARON and LOTTE enter from dinner. GERTRUDE carries an evening bag. A small side table has been added against the Downstage Right wall.

GERTRUDE. Dinner was absolutely superb. The weinerschnitzel and sauerbraten were perfection and the potato dumplings, so delectable. I will not leave without your mother's recipe. (*Sits on the sofa.*)

BARON. I am so happy you enjoyed your last supper ... before you leave us. Is there no way, my darling, I can persuade you to stay? (*Sits next to Gertrude on the sofa.*)

GERTRUDE. I'm afraid not. When MGM calls, one lifts one's skirts and runs. Just imagine, me starring as myself in my own musical biography, "I Love a Piano." Of course, I am heartbroken I had to cancel my concert at the Festspielhaus. All those poor little burghers who camped out all night to buy their tickets.

LOTTE. But what of your friend, the Countess, what if she returns and you're not here?

GERTRUDE. (*Holding herself together.*) I'm sure wherever she is, she will understand.

BARON. She left without saying goodbye.

DOKTOR. An enchanting creature. (*Crosses to fireplace and lights a cigarette.*)

BARON. But you, Gertrude, when will I see you again?

GERTRUDE. I shall be in Los Angeles through December. I'm sure by then, darling, you and your men will be marching down La Cienega Boulevard.

DOKTOR. I am so disappointed. I did so want to show you my laboratory. I am just beginning with human experiments.

GERTRUDE. I am fascinated by science. Music is, after all, closely allied to the field of physics.

BARON. Perhaps, Herr Doktor, Gertrude will stay if we, how do you Americans say, twist her arm.

LOTTE. I'll twist her arm, uncle.

THE LADY IN QUESTION 87

GERTRUDE. Dear Lotte, I do hope some day you'll realize that you have a special kind of beauty, the kind which comes from within, my precious little monkeyface.

(AUGUSTA enters with a tray of strudel, through the kitchen's swinging doors. SHE places it on the small table against the Downstage Right wall.)

AUGUSTA. I have a surprise for our lovely guest. I have baked my famous Von Elsner strudel.

BARON. Oh, Mother, you haven't. Gertrude, we have a great treat in store for us.

GERTRUDE. Oh, dear. Had I but known. The sauerbraten did me in.

LOTTE. This strudel will really do you in.

GERTRUDE. My girdle is way too tight already.

AUGUSTA. Just a small piece, a sliver.

GERTRUDE. I couldn't.

BARON. Mother shall be quite offended.

AUGUSTA. I shall be furious.

GERTRUDE. I'll take a sliver.

AUGUSTA. The pieces are already cut, so you just eat as much as you can. *(Puts powdered sugar on Gertrude's strudel.)*

DOKTOR. Augusta, *I* am furious. Never once have you baked me your famous strudel.

AUGUSTA. (*Serving everyone.*) Tut, tut, tut, Herr Doktor. When your first human experiment survives, I shall make you my all-butter pound cake. (*Gives Gertrude her specially prepared piece of strudel.*) Eat up, dear. See if it is to your taste.

GERTRUDE. (*Innocently perplexed.*) Why is mine the only piece with powdered sugar?

AUGUSTA. I ... I understood all Americans liked things sweet. Should I take it off?

GERTRUDE. No. It looks divine.

(*THEY all stare at her.*)

GERTRUDE. (*Takes a bite and grimaces with revulsion then tries to be polite.*) Mmmm, light as air.

BARON. Mother, you must have worked hours on that strudel.

LOTTE. And I helped.

AUGUSTA. Indeed she did. Lotte was my chancellor of ingredients. And she was most precise, everything according to measure.

(*GERTRUDE is gradually growing sicker.*)

DOKTOR. That powdered sugar looks good.

BARON. Careful, Max. You don't want a potbelly.

DOKTOR. I don't care. Madame Garnet, if you don't mind, I shall be quite boorish and take a little of that powdered sugar.

(*GERTRUDE holds out her plate and the DOKTOR's fork is going for the sugar ...*)

BARON.	AUGUSTA.
(*Alarmed.*) That's for Ger ...	(*Fiercely.*) No, Max ... sweets are not good for you.

(*The DOKTOR pulls back his fork and GERTRUDE realizes there's poison in the sugar. SHE looks at the Doktor.*)

GERTRUDE. (*Elegantly.*) Excuse me. (*She gives her plate to Baron.*) Excuse me. (*SHE leans over the back of the sofa and violently throws it all up. The OTHERS quickly get out of the way.*)

GERTRUDE. I guess it didn't agree with me.
AUGUSTA. You have not fooled us, Fraülein Garnet.

(*DOKTOR crosses to a lever against the Upstage Left wall and pulls it up. A strong "interrogation" LIGHT hits Gertrude on the sofa.*)

BARON. Mother, let me handle this. Gertrude, you will tell us everything you know about Raina Aldric.

GERTRUDE. She's a great actress.

BARON. Tell me more.

GERTRUDE. I believe she made a silent film in 'twenty-six.

BARON. (*Barks.*) Do not be flippant! You have taken me for an idiot, but no more. Your life is in my hands. Raina Aldric has escaped her prison. You have helped her. Who are your confederates?

GERTRUDE. (*Terrified.*) I don't know what you're talking about.

AUGUSTA. Your friend, Kitty, she knew, didn't she?

GERTRUDE. (*Emotionally.*) You tell me, since I'm sure you were the last to see her alive.

BARON. Where is Raina Aldric now? Tell me the truth!

GERTRUDE. (*Fighting for composure.*) I don't know where she is. Never met the dame.

DOKTOR. Where is Raina Aldric?

GERTRUDE. (*Assuming a tough facade.*) Don't you guys lissen? I told you I know nothing about that old lady. Got my own troubles, and if Goering, Goebbels and Himmler asked me, I'd tell 'em the same. And get that light out of my eyes. What are you fitting me for, glasses?

AUGUSTA. We will be fitting you for a coffin if you do not comply.

GERTRUDE. Testy.

BARON. Why should you be so loyal to your country? I thought you considered yourself a citizen of the world, Madame Gertrude Gar*net* (*Gar-nay.*)

GERTRUDE. The name's Gertie Garnet (*In the American pronunciation.*) I'm a citizen of Brooklyn, New York.

DOKTOR. Brooklyn?

GERTRUDE. Yeah, what's it to you?

BARON. This Brooklyn, it will soon be part of the Third Reich.

GERTRUDE. (*With defiant pride.*) Brother, you may take the Maginot Line, but you'll never take the Canarsie Line.

AUGUSTA. Your bravado is quite pathetic.

GERTRUDE. I give as good as I get.

DOKTOR. You will tell us the truth. I have several medical methods that can be most excruciating.

GERTRUDE. All right, I'll give you some truth. This whole set up in Germany stinks. And your Führer, Herr Hitler, has only one nut to his name.

AUGUSTA. (*In a rage.*) Damn you! Damn you!!!

BARON. Mother, control yourself.

AUGUSTA. (*With mad fervor.*) That is a filthy lie. The Führer has two enormous testicles!!

BARON. I believe this is time to call in our next subject. Doktor Maximilian, have Karel bring in the young lady.
GERTRUDE. Please don't.

(*The DOKTOR pulls down the lever, killing the LIGHT. HE calls for "Karel!" KAREL enters with HEIDI and pushes her towards the fireplace. KAREL stands behind the sofa.*)

BARON. Good evening, Miss Mittelhoffer. So happy you could join us. Please answer a few questions, and then we shall release you. Where is Raina Aldric?
HEIDI. (*Lying very badly.*) I know nothing. Please, believe me.
BARON. Come, child, do not fear us. We will not harm you. Where have you taken her?
HEIDI. I know nothing. Please let me go.
BARON. You are guilty of hideous crimes against the Reich. You will tell us everything.
AUGUSTA. Let me. (*SHE crosses for a cigar.*) Miss Mittelhoffer. Do you mind if I call you Heidi? Pardon my indulgence. There's nothing I like better than a good after-dinner cigar. So fragrant. So satisfying. (*Holds the lit cigar close to Heidi's face.*) Tell me, girl, where is Raina Aldric?
HEIDI. Believe me. I don't know where she is.
AUGUSTA. You are very pretty. I can make it so no man will ever love you.

HEIDI. (*Near hysterics.*) Please believe me. I don't know anything.

(*AUGUSTA, frustrated, crosses the stage growling animal-like.*)

LOTTE. Karel, you're very quiet. Karel and Miss Mittelhoffer are very old friends. Perhaps Karel will have some influence on her.
KAREL. We are mere acquaintances.
LOTTE. (*Viciously.*) That's not true. I believe they were once sweethearts.
BARON. Who is your allegiance to? This tramp or the Führer?
KAREL. The Führer, Herr Baron.
BARON. Then rip off her blouse. Rip it off, I command you.

(*KAREL rips off her blouse, revealing her chemise.*)

BARON. Mother, the whip.

(*AUGUSTA gets whip from table and gives it to the Baron.*)

BARON. Doktor, please escort Mother to the library. Lotte, go to your room. This is not for your eyes.
LOTTE. Oh drat, just when the fun starts.

(*AUGUSTA and the DOKTOR exit Upstage Left. LOTTE runs upstairs and exits.*)

BARON. (*Handing whip to Karel.*) Karel, give her five lashes and perhaps her memory will serve her better.
KAREL. (*Tortured.*) Yes, Herr Baron.
GERTRUDE. (*Rushing to the Baron.*) Please! The girl is innocent. She has been told nothing.
BARON. Silence!!! Proceed, Karel.

(*KAREL places HEIDI's hands on the mantle of the fireplace to steady her and hesitantly starts to whip her. Each time he hits her the BARON yells, "Harder." Although SHE screams at each strike, SHE is being very brave. On the last one SHE falls to the floor sobbing. KAREL is in a state of shock.*)

BARON. Once more, tell me, girl, where is Raina Aldric?
HEIDI. (*With raw, ugly power.*) You can all rot in *hell!!!*
BARON. How defiant and most entertaining. I am in the mood for more entertainment. Karel, I would like to see you and this young lady have sexual intercourse. Here, before us. Karel, rape her.
KAREL. Please, Baron, do not force me to do this.
BARON. You must do this for the Führer.

KAREL. I can't. I won't! Have you no respect for human life?

BARON. Karel, watch yourself.

KAREL. (*Takes out a gun and points it at the Baron.*) No, watch yourself. I though you were a great man. How wrong I was, you are a monster. Heidi, put on your blouse, we're going.

(*LOTTE enters from upstairs.*)

BARON. Where are you going? You fool, traitor!

LOTTE. (*Runs down the stairs.*) Karel, you're leaving. You're leaving together. You can't do that. You can't do that! I won't let you!

KAREL. Don't come any closer!

LOTTE. (*Feverishly.*) I'm the one you desire.

BARON. (*Aghast.*) Lotte, what are you saying?

LOTTE. Ravage me, impale me!

KAREL. Get out of my way.

LOTTE. Fuck me, Karel, fuck me! (*Insane.*) You don't want her. I'll get her out of the way. I'll kill her for you. This will be the test of my love.

(*SHE pulls out a knife and is about to stab Heidi when KAREL shoots her and SHE falls dead.*)

KAREL. (*Drops the gun on the sofa in disgust.*) Come, Heidi.

(*THEY run out the front door.*)

BARON. (*With mad vengeance.*) The traitors, they will not go far. I shall phone the Gestapo and put an end to this ridiculous love story.

GERTRUDE. (*Picks up the gun on the sofa and points it at him.*) Put down that phone.

BARON. I certainly will not.

GERTRUDE. Put it down, I say.

BARON. Give me the gun. You do not have the courage to fire it.

GERTRUDE. Oh, don't I? (*Defiant MUSIC comes in.*) What a joy it will be to kill you. Yes, joy. But first I shall torture you as you have tortured thousands. You thought I loved you. I never loved you. I pitied you because you were a pathetic, mother-fixated fool. Imagine my happiness when I execute you and escape with my lover. Yes, my handsome, young lover. You, who hounded an innocent actress nearly to her death. You, who cruelly humiliated a pair of young lovers. You, who murdered my friend. The Lord God in Heaven may forgive you but I never shall. Now die, your excellency, die.

BARON. Gertie, perhaps I was a trifle brusque.

(*SHE pushes him up the stairs.*)

BARON. (*Pathetically yellow.*) You are a great artist, artists should be above such nonsense as politics. Gertie, don't shoot. I beg of you. I don't wanna die. I'll do anything. I'll make any phone call. I have money. You want cash? How much, take it, a hundred marks? Don't, Gertie, don't. Mother! Mother! Don't shoot.

(*SHE impassively SHOOTS him twice, then once more as an afterthought. The MUSIC fades out.*)

GERTRUDE. (*With bitter irony.*) And to think, before you, once trembled all of Schauffehausen.
ERIK. (*Runs in from the library.*) Gertie, are you all right? What happened?
GERTRUDE. (*Terribly shaken.*) I killed him. I killed him.
ERIK. We must get Mother out. The car will be here any minute.
GERTRUDE. What about the Baroness and the Doktor? Shan't they hear us?
ERIK. Dr. Maximilian saw me climbing in through the window. We thrashed it out and I've got him tied-up in the basement.
GERTRUDE. And the Baroness ...?
ERIK. (*Lights a cigarette at the mantle.*) She heard us fighting and came after me with a shovel. I belted her in the stomach, got her in a half-Nelson, and wrestled her to the ground.

Then I grabbed her by the hair and dragged her across the room and slammed her against an old chifferobe. When she was knocked out cold, I tied her to the Doktor. They'll keep for awhile. Professor Mittelhoffer!

(*The PROFESSOR comes in from the front door. ERIK puts out the cigarette.*)

PROFESSOR. I heard shooting. Was Heidi here? (*Sees the bodies.*) Ach du leiber.
GERTRUDE. They brought her in and tortured her. You'd have been proud. They couldn't break her spirit. Karel saved her and got her out of the house. He's on our side now.
PROFESSOR. She is a smart girl, she knows to meet us outside the servants' entrance at midnight. It's almost time.
ERIK. Let's go get Mother.

(*RAINA enters from the upstairs right room, walking slowly. She is wearing a fur coat and looks radiant.*)

ERIK. Mother, you're walking. (*HE starts for her.*)
RAINA. (*With great courage.*) Don't help me. I must walk to freedom on my own two legs!

(*THEY embrace on the stairs.*)

PROFESSOR. Oh dear, with Karel along, we don't have enough letters of transit. What should we do?

GERTRUDE. Then you must take mine. (*Gets her purse from sofa.*)

ERIK. We couldn't. You'd never get out.

GERTRUDE. I'd find a way. I always do.

ERIK. (*Crossing to the mantle.*) We're close to the Swiss border. We could possibly make it by foot.

GERTRUDE. But you, you have a letter of transit.

ERIK. It means nothing without you. I'll take my chance with you in the mountains.

PROFESSOR. It's midnight. I think I hear the car.

RAINA. Bless you, Gertrude. You have given me back my life, my son and my art. "Gallop apace, you fiery-footed steeds ..."

PROFESSOR. Come, Raina, the plane leaves promptly in ten minutes.

GERTRUDE. Here is your letter of transit, Madame Aldric, and you can't greet your public without this. (*Gives her a lipstick.*)

RAINA. A lipstick, and such a lovely color. (*Puts it on; kisses Gertrude's hands.*) Thank you, thank you, thank you.

(*GERTRUDE gives her the handbag.*)

ERIK. Mother, I'll meet you across the border.

(THEY kiss.)

ERIK. Professor, good luck.

(RAINA and the PROFESSOR exit.)

GERTRUDE. Darling, there's still time. You should have gone with them. I'll never forgive myself if you ...
ERIK. Shhhh.

(THEY listen to the outside. We hear the CAR drive off.)

ERIK. They're on their way.
GERTRUDE. What do we do now? How do we find Switzerland?
ERIK. We have very simple directions. I'll show you.

(HE takes her hands and leads her to the open door. THEY look out.)

ERIK. We just follow that brightest star. Are you game?

GERTRUDE. I love an adventure.
ERIK. Let's go.

FADE TO BLACK

(*Lush, romantic MUSIC redolent of courageous adventure comes in and eventually underscores the following voice over.*)

ACT II

Scene 3

In the blackout, we hear ...

VOICE-OVER. Flash. Flash. Dateline Bavaria. Famed U.S. piano virtuoso, Gertrude Garnet, is missing and feared dead after aiding the escape of German stage actress, Raina Aldric, from a Nazi prison. Miss Aldric and companions have landed safely in Zurich but fear Nazi retaliation against Miss Garnet and against Miss Aldric's son, Erik Maxwell. Stay tuned for further reports.

(*The large screen from Scene 1 is across the stage. LIGHTS come up on the Right side of the screen detailing a mountain landscape. On grooves carved into the screen, two small FIGURINES representing Gertrude and Erik are seen skiing down the mountain. The effect should be that of a movie "long shot." This is accompanied by thrilling, adventure MUSIC. The LIGHTS fade down and rise on the Left side of the stage where GERTRUDE and ERIK are seen in person skiing on a small slope. SNOW is falling on them and loud GUNSHOTS are heard in rapid succession.*)

GERTRUDE. (*Skiing.*) Faster, darling, faster!

ERIK. Where'd you learn to ski?

GERTRUDE. San Moritz, Vail and Aspen. They're shooting at us!

ERIK. Don't look back! When we get back to the states, will you marry me?

GERTRUDE. Of course, darling. I think I'd make a divine professor's wife. And when I go on tour during summer vacation, will you join me?

ERIK. I'll carry all the luggage.

GERTRUDE. Then you've got yourself a deal. Are we almost there?

ERIK. I can't tell in this darkness.

(*A SHOT rings out and hits ERIK in the back. HE falls to the ground. GERTRUDE stops skiing and joins him on the ground. The MUSIC and SNOW fade out.*)

GERTRUDE. Erik! Erik!
ERIK. Keep going!
GERTRUDE. I will not. You're hurt. Hold onto me!
ERIK. (*Through his pain.*) No, go ahead. I'll catch up with you.
GERTRUDE. (*With great emotion.*) Darling, if this is the way it ends, so be it. During these past few days, you've taught me more than most people learn in a lifetime.
ERIK. (*Fading away.*) I can hardly see your face.
GERTRUDE. (*Desperately.*) Hold onto me, darling. (*With great determination.*) No one's going to harm you.

(*The end seems to be near. Wistful, quietly sad MUSIC is heard.*)

GERTRUDE. Erik, what a fool I've been. All these years I've been obsessed with myself and called it a philosophy. (*Very simply and with great restraint.*) This is what matters. This is real. Fighting for something I believe in. Loving someone. Why must we always come to our senses when it's too late? (*SHE pauses and realizes there is silence.*) Listen, the shooting has stopped. Do you hear?

(*ERIK lifts himself up to a somewhat seated position. He's going to live. The MUSIC becomes more hopeful.*)

ERIK. Yes, the night is suddenly peaceful.
GERTRUDE. (*Pointing to the sky.*) Look, darling, the brightest star. It's directly over our heads. We must have crossed the border! (*Elated.*) We're free, darling, we're free! (*Eyes full of tears, SHE's the embodiment of bravery as she cradles Erik in her arms. Her voice rises in emotional rhythm and cadence.*) And soon that bright star will shine above all of Europe, and the whole world will glow in its radiance, brighter and stronger than we've ever, ever known!

(*The MUSIC builds triumphantly as the LIGHTS fade out on GERTRUDE and ERIK's upturned, enraptured faces. Above them, we see the snow-capped mountains and the title "The End" appears as if through the clouds.*)

FADE TO BLACK

COSTUME PLOT

GERTRUDE GARNET

Act I, Sc. 1

Black hat with raven feathers and blue beading; Periwinkle blue two-piece traveling suit with black fur trim at hem of skirt; Black fur stole; Black gloves; Black purse; Black heels; Rhinestone earbobs and matching brooch; Red wig with large forties pompadour and rolled under in the back.

Act I, Sc. 2

Ecru crepe evening gown with gold lame beaded military collar, epaulets, cuffs, midriff and underskirt; Bone evening heels; Flowing red wig with pompadour.

Act I, Sc. 3

White blouse; Red, green and blue plaid taffeta wrap-vest; Forest green wool skirt; Black heels; Repeat wig from Sc. 2; Pearl earrings

Act I, Sc. 5

White blouse; Ecru riding jacket with pocket crest; Brown jodhpurs; Brown boots; Brown and ecru print ascot; Shoulder length simple red wig worn throughout the rest of the play.

Act II, Sc. 1

Dark violet dressing gown; Pale lavender organza underskirt; Black heels.

Act II, Sc. 2

Black & white zebra print silk crepe evening blouse; Black crepe-backed satin evening pants; Wide black sequin stretch belt; Black heels; Rhinestone eardrops and bracelet.

Act II, Sc. 3

Add striped fawn and white fur parka.

KITTY

Act I, Sc. 1

Dark navy hat with polka dot tulle drape and red birds; Dark red two-piece suit with brown fur shoulder collar; Brown fur muff; Pink

THE LADY IN QUESTION 107

gloves, Black heels, Rhinestone eardrops, necklace, rings; Blonde shoulder length wig.

Act I, Sc. 2

Fuschia "harem" hat with pink sparkle chiffon drape; Fuschia crepe evening gown with pink sparkle chiffon shoulder and hip drapes; Pink evening gloves, fuschia heels.

Act I, Sc. 3

Pink crepe blouse with hood; Corsage of violets; Burgundy plaid skirt; Black heels.

Act I, Sc. 4

Add print scarf with scarf ring.

AUGUSTA

Act I, Sc. 2

Grey fur hat with black jacquard cowl; Black wool dress coat with grey fur sleeves; Black velvet cape with jet beading and grey fur trim; Black gloves, heels, jet bracelet; Pale grey pompadour wig showing in front of hat.

Act I, Sc. 5

Black crepe dress with black sequin embroidery; Black lace fringed shawl; Black heels; Pale grey pompadour wig.

Act II, Sc. 1

Add black full-length cape with velvet collar.

Act II, Sc. 2

Black lace gown (*to overdress last costume*); Rhinestone snake pin; Black lace mitts.

RAINA

Act I, Sc. 3

Lavender nightgown (distressed)

Act II, Sc. 1

Repeat.

Act II, Sc. 2

Add fur coat.

LOTTE

Act I, Sc. 2

Ecru puff-sleeved blouse; Black velvet waistcoat with embroidered shoulder straps; Apple green linen skirt with fuschia lace and embroidered ribbon trim; Pink knee socks; Black pumps; Blonde wig with bangs and two braids.

Act I, Sc. 4

Repeat.

Act II, Sc. 1

Black velvet bodice with gold rose appliques and pale green organza puff sleeves; Pale green organza skirt with black lace trim; Pink ruffle petticoat; White tights; Black pumps.

Act II, Sc. 2

Repeat.

HEIDI

Act I, Sc. 1

Dark green alpine hat; White blouse; Pink skirt; Brown wool coat with plaid collar and cuffs; Pale pink anklets; Brown pumps, Shoulder length dark brown wig.

Act I, Sc. 3

Pale grey headscarf; Olive green uniform dress with Nazi shoulder patch; Patch grey bib apron; Black pumps.

Act II, Sc. 2

White break-away blouse with pink floral trim; White camisole; Pink skirt; Pale pink anklets; Brown pumps; Gold locket

BARON

Act I, Sc. 1

Officer's cap; White shirt; Dk. green tie; Grey-green officer's overcoat; Grey-green Jodhpurs; Black "Sam Browne" belt with holster; Black riding boots.

Act I, Sc. 2

Remove cap, overcoat and belt; Add grey-green officer's tunic.

Act II, Sc. 1

Dark green dress tunic with medals & gold epaulets; Dark red Baldric with gold braid and fringe; Black dress pants;

Act II, Sc. 2

Repeat.

HUGO

Act I, Sc. 1

Grey tweed cap; White striped shirt; Dark brown pants; Print necktie; Grey-brown tweed overcoat; Dk. red sweater vest; Dk. brown socks; Black shoes.

PROFESSOR

Act I, Sc. 1

Brown homburg; White shirt/wing-tip collar; Print bowtie; Grey pants with suspenders; Socks; Black shoes; Purple-grey overcoat; Wire rim glasses; Grey moustache.

Repeats throughout rest of play.

DOKTOR

Act I, Sc. 2

Black pin-stripe double-breasted suit; White shirt; Dk. red tie; Nazi armband; Black socks; Black shoes

ERIK

Act I, Sc. 1

Grey fedora; Cream shirt; Cream, rust & grey print tie; Brown tweed three-piece suit; Brown socks; Brown shoes; Dk. grey trenchcoat.

Act I, Sc. 2

Remove hat and trenchcoat.

Act II, Sc. 1

Dark blue double-breasted suit with matching vest; Dark blue tie; Pale blue shirt; Black socks; Black shoes.

Act II, Sc. 3

Remove coat and vest; Add brown leather jacket.

KAREL

Act I, Sc. 1

Brown visored cap; Brown uniform shirt; Brown tie; Brown short jacket; Nazi armband; Brown "Sam Browne" belt with holster; Brown pants; Brown riding boots

Wears this uniform throughout play.

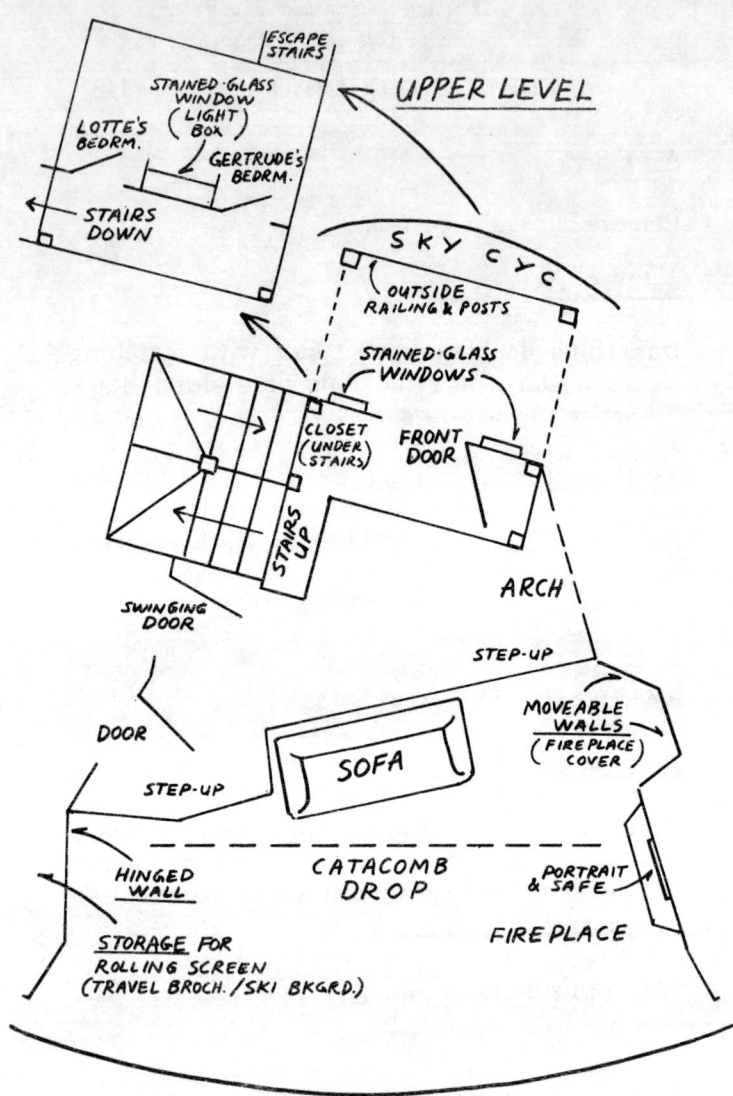

SET DESIGN
"THE LADY IN QUESTION"

(COURTESY: BT Whitehill...)

Other Publications for Your Interest

HUNTING COCKROACHES
(LITTLE THEATRE—COMEDY)

By JANUSZ GLOWACKI
Translated by JADWIGA KOSICKA

7 men, 2 women—Doubling possible Int. setting.

New York's Manhattan Theatre Club had a hit with this delightfully offbeat comedy, directed by Arthur Penn and starring Oscar-winner Dianne Wiest. This is a play about a contemporary immigrant couple from Poland named Jan and Anka, who are having quite a time coping with their strange new country. Anka, once a well-known classical actress in Warsaw, can't get work over here because of her accent; while Jan, a writer, struggles with a titanic case of writer's block. As they try valiantly to get some sleep late one night, they cope with various "flash-backs", in which characters from their past come crawling out from underneath their bed. These include a thick-headed U.S. Immigration official, a street bum, a well-meaning wealthy Park Avenue couple and two guys from Warsaw trying to get their apartment back home. "An extremely funny and exhilarating play."—Newhouse Newsp. "Mordantly funny...salted with the kind of observations that make us laugh."—Newsday. "A quintessentially brash, delightful play."—NY Times. "One of the funniest comedies I have seen in years."—NY Post.

(#10166)

CINDERS
(LITTLE THEATRE—COMIC DRAMA)

By JANUSZ GLOWACKI
Translated by CHRISTINA PAUL
Music by RICHARD PEASLEE

7 men, 8 women—Various int. sets (may be unit set).

The New York Shakespeare Festival had quite a success with this penetrating allegory about a totalitarian police state by a Polish dissident playwright and novelist. In a reform school for girls, near Warsaw, a documentary film director plans to do a film of the school's production of the classic "Cinderella". The authorities of the school welcome his arrival, as they believe his film will show the world how enlightened the state can be in its institutions of social welfare. The director plans to create a documentary whose theme is how innocent children are rescued from the web of society. When the girl playing Cinderella refuses to participate in this phoney charade, both the director and the school authorities collaborate in her punishment. "One can only admire the author's will to make elegant Kafkaesque comedy out of his nation's nightmare of repression...If topsy-turvey language is the comic currency of *Cinders*, the play's drama derives from the warping of souls as much as words."—NY Times.
(#5071)

Other Publications for Your Interest

THE CURATE SHAKESPEARE AS YOU LIKE IT
(LITTLE THEATRE—COMEDY)

By DON NIGRO

4 men, 3 women—Bare stage

This extremely unusual and original piece is subtitled: "The record of one company's attempt to perform the play by William Shakespeare". When the very prolific Mr. Nigro was asked by a professional theatre company to adapt *As You Like It* so that it could be performed by a company of seven he, of course, came up with a completely original play about a rag-tag group of players comprised of only seven actors led by a dotty old curate who nonetheless must present Shakespeare's play; and the dramatic interest, as well as the comedy, is in their hilarious attempts to impersonate all of Shakespeare's multitude of characters. The play has had numerous productions nationwide, all of which have come about through word of mouth. We are very pleased to make this "underground comic classic" widely available to theatre groups who like their comedy wide open and theatrical. (#5742)

SEASCAPE WITH SHARKS AND DANCER
(LITTLE THEATRE—DRAMA)

By DON NIGRO

1 man, 1 woman—Interior

This is a fine new play by an author of great talent and promise. We are very glad to be introducing Mr. Nigro's work to a wide audience with *Seascape With Sharks and Dancer*, which comes directly from a sold-out, critically acclaimed production at the world-famous Oregon Shakespeare Festival. The play is set in a beach bungalow. The young man who lives there has pulled a lost young woman from the ocean. Soon, she finds herself trapped in his life and torn between her need to come to rest somewhere and her certainty that all human relationships turn eventually into nightmares. The struggle between his tolerant and gently ironic approach to life and her strategy of suspicion and attack becomes a kind of war about love and creation which neither can afford to lose. In other words, this is quite an offbeat, wonderful love story. We would like to point out that the play also contains a wealth of excellent ***monologue*** and ***scene material.*** (#21060)

Other Publications for Your Interest

THE ROCKY HORROR SHOW
(MUSICAL)
Book, music and lyrics by RICHARD O'BRIEN

7 men, 3 women. Various ints. and exts.

At last! The original stage version of the cult movie that has been a "12 O'clock high " for thousands of enthusiastic movie-goers. Live, on stage, see Dr. Frank N. Furter match wits (?) with the innocent young newlyweds! Thrill to the delightfully trashy rock and roll music! "It isn't a play, it isn't a musical, it isn't a rock concert...It's a sort of glitter, rock, horror, comedy, tranvestite circus...And if you love—say, 'Sound of Music'—you will probably hate it."—WABC-TV. "*The Rocky Horror Show* is a sicko-wacko-weirdo rock concert. It keeps trying to blow your mind with loud music and perverted sexuality, but it is so simple-minded, and so completely silly, that it ends up being a lot of fun. It may get a cult following, even though there is no nudity."—NBC.
(#20049)

(Restricted. When available, Terms quoted on application—Music available on rental.) Posters Available

VAMPIRE LESBIANS OF SODOM
(ADVENTUROUS GROUPS.) FARCE
By CHARLES BUSCH

6 men, 2 women. Unit set

This truly bizarre entertainment, cut right out of the *Rocky Horror* genre, is about vamps, has nothing to do with lesbians and takes the audience from ancient Sodom to the Hollywood of the twenties, ending up somehow in present day Las Vegas. "Costumes flashier than pinball machines, outrageous lines, awful puns, sinister innocence, harmless depravity—it's all here. One can imagine a cult forming."—NY Times. "Bizarre and wonderful...If you think Boy George is a gender-bender, well, like Jolson said, you ain't seen nothing yet! Forget your genders, come on, get happy."—Broadway Mag. Published with *Sleeping Beauty, or Coma*. (Royalty, $50-$40.) (#24006)

Other Publications for Your Interest

I'M NOT RAPPAPORT
(LITTLE THEATRE—COMEDY)
By HERB GARDNER

5 men, 2 women—Exterior

Just when we thought there would never be another joyous, laugh-filled evening on Broadway, along came this delightful play to restore our faith in the Great White Way. If you thought *A Thousand Clowns* was wonderful, wait til you take a look at *I'm Not Rappaport!* Set in a secluded spot in New York's Central Park, the play is about two octogenarians determined to fight off all attempts to put them out to pasture. Talk about an odd couple! Nat is a lifelong radical determined to fight injustice (real or imagined) who is also something of a spinner of fantasies. He has a delightful repertoire of eccentric personas, which makes the role an actor's dream. The other half of this unlikely partnership is Midge, a Black apartment super who spends his days in the park hiding out from tenants, who want him to retire. "Rambunctiously funny."—N.Y. Post. "A warm and entertaining evening."—W.W. Daily. **Tony Award Winner, Best Play 1986. Posters.**

(#11071)

CROSSING DELANCEY
(LITTLE THEATRE—COMEDY)
By SUSAN SANDLER

2 men, 3 women—Comb. Interior/Exterior.

Isabel is a young Jewish woman who lives alone and works in a NYC bookshop. When she is not pining after a handsome author who is one of her best customers, she is visiting her grandmother—who lives by herself in the "old neighborhood", Manhattan's Lower East Side. Isabel is in no hurry to get married, which worries her grandmother. The delightfully nosey old lady hires an old friend who is—can you believe this in the 1980's?—a matchmaker. Bubbie and the matchmaker come up with a Good Catch for their Isabel—Sam, a young pickle vendor. Same is no *schlemiel*, though. He likes Isabel; but he knows he is going to have to woo her, which he proceeds to do. When Isabel realizes what a cad the author is, and what a really nice man Sam is, she begins to respond; and the end of the play is really a beginning, ripe with possibilities for Isabel and "An amusing interlude for theatregoers who may have thought that simple romance and sentimentality had long since been relegated to television sitcoms...tells its unpretentious story believeably, rarely trying to make its gag lines, of which there are many, upstage its narration or outshine its heart."—N.Y. Times. "A warm and loving drama...a welcome addition to the growing body of Jewish dramatic work in this country."—Jewish Post and Opinion.

(#5739)

Other Publications for Your Interest

EMERALD CITY
(LITTLE THEATRE—COMEDY)

By DAVID WILLIAMSON
(author of the screenplays to "The Year of Living Dangerously" and Gallipoli")

3 men, 3 women—Unit set

In "the trade"—i.e., the movie biz as covered by *Variety*—"Oz" is not over the rainbow but Down Under. Australia. Which makes Sydney the Emerald City, where there is not one wizard but a host of them, who are the Deal-Makers. Colin, a critically-praised but commercially under-successful screenwriter, and his wife Kate, an Editor, feel a change of venue is called for, from Melbourne (i.e., The Sticks) to Sydney, the Emerald City, the major leagues. There, Colin joins forces with an aggressive, fast-talking aspiring screenwriter named Mike, who has no discernible talent for writing but who is a genius at the Art of the Deal. Mike parlays his tenuous connection with Colin into a series of cinematic projects which culminate in his becoming a global tycoon, a pinnacle from which he can put many different projects into "development", such as Kate's pet project, a serious aboriginal novel, which Mike plans to transplant to Tennessee as a vehicle for Eddie Murphy. Eventually, Colin and Kate must make a moral decision: is the Emerald City a sane place to be: or do they want to go back to Kansas? "Hype and Hypocrisy amusingly help to speed the plow on the road to *Emerald City.*"—N.Y. Times. "Winsomely cynical."—Time Mag. "Funny and engaging...his characters must be as much fun to play as they are to listen to." —N.Y. Post. "An incisive, grimly graceful, painfully funny play...this examination of how the noble ambition for fame deteriorates into lust for money and power, and how relationships of every kind subsist on deception, deserves our delightedly undivided attention. *Emerald City* portrays human rivalry with maximum comic and dramatic effect because it is as humorous as it is witty."—N.Y. Mag.

(#7078)

THE FILM SOCIETY
(LITTLE THEATRE—DRAMATIC COMEDY

By JON ROBIN BAITZ

4 men, 2 women—Various interiors. (may be unit set).

Imagine the best of Simon Gray crossed with the best of Athol Fugard. The New York critics lavished praise upon this wonderful play, calling Mr. Baitz a major new voice in our theatre. *The Film Society*, set in South Africa, is *not* about the effects of apartheid—at least, overtly. Blenheim is a provincial private school modeled on the second-rate British education machine. It is 1970, a time of complacency for everyone but Terry, a former teacher at Blenheim, who has lost his job because of his connections with Blacks (he invited a Black priest to speak at Commencement). Terry tries to involve Jonathan, another teacher at the school and the central character in this play; but Jonathan cares only about his film society, which he wants to keep going at all costs—even if it means programming only safe, non-objectionable, films. When Jonathan's mother, a local rich lady, promises to donate a substantial amount of money to Blenheim if Jonathan is made Headmaster, he must finally choose which side he is on: Terry's or The Establishment's. "Using the school of a microcosm for South Africa, Baitz explores the psychological workings of repression in a society that has to kill its conscience in order to persist in a course of action it knows enough to abhor but cannot afford to relinquish."—New Yorker. "What distinguishes Mr. Baitz' writing, aside from its manifest literacy, is its ability to embrace the ambiguities of political and moral dilemmas that might easily be reduced to blacks and whites."—N.Y. Times. "A beautiful, accomplished play...things I thought I was a churl still to value or expect—things like character, plot and theatre dialogue—really do matter."—N.Y. Daily News.

(#8123)

Other Publications for Your Interest

CINDERELLA WALTZ
(ALL GROUPS—COMEDY)

By DON NIGRO

4 men, 5 women—1 set

Rosey Snow is trapped in a fairy tale world that is by turns funny and a little frightening, with her stepsisters Goneril and Regan, her demented stepmother, her lecherous father, a bewildered Prince, a fairy godmother who sings salty old sailor songs, a troll and a possibly homicidal village idiot. A play which investigates the archetypal origins of the world's most popular fairy tale and the tension between the more familiar and charming Perrault version and the darker, more ancient and disturbing tale recorded by the brothers Grimm. Grotesque farce and romantic fantasy blend in a fairy tale for adults.

(#5208)

ROBIN HOOD
(LITTLE THEATRE—COMEDY)

By DON NIGRO

14 men, 8 women—(more if desired.) Unit set.

In a land where the rich get richer, the poor are starving, and Prince John wants to cut down Sherwood Forest to put up an arms manufactory, a slaughterhouse and a tennis court for the well to do, this bawdy epic unites elements of wild farce and ancient popular mythologies with an environmentalist assault on the arrogance of wealth and power in the face of poverty and hunger. Amid feeble and insane jesters, a demonic snake oil salesman, a corrupt and lascivious court, a singer of eerie ballads, a gluttonous lusty friar and a world of vivid and grotesque characters out of a Brueghel painting, Maid Marian loses her clothes and her illusions among the poor and Robin tries to avoid murder and elude the Dark Monk of the Wood who is Death and also perhaps something more.

(#20075)